The High Cost of Doing Nothing

The High Cost of Doing Nothing

By Hank Moore
Futurist, Corporate Strategist™

Skyward Publishing, Inc.

Publisher: Skyward Publishing, Inc. Marketing
813 Michael Street
Kennett, MO 63857
Phone 573-717-1040
Fax: 413-702-5141
Email: skyward@sheltonbbs.com
Web Site: www.skywardpublishing.com

Library of Congress Cataloging-in-Publication Data
Moore, Hank

The high cost of doing nothing: why good companies go bad, how to avoid troubles and assure success, painting the big picture of business success, corporate mentor's body of knowledge/by Hank Moore.

p.cm.—(Business library anthology series)

Includes bibliographical references.

ISBN 1-881554-21-X

1.Industrial management 2. Business failures. 3. Corporate turnarounds. 4. Success in business. I Title. II. Series.

HD31.M6254 2002
658-dc21

2001049568

ATTENTION SCHOOLS AND CORPORATIONS

Contents

Foreword

How organizations start out and what they become are decidedly different concepts. Mistakes, niche orientation and lack of planning lead businesses to failure. This book views the whole of the organization, then the parts and back to the sum.

Hank Moore, Futurist and Corporate Strategist™ , developed this trademarked concept over the last 20 years, applying it to many of his 2,000 clients (from small businesses to Fortune 500 corporations to the public sector to non-profit organizations). All clients agreed that no road map was initially laid out for them.

Executives have amassed their business knowledge "in the streets," through non-traditional sources. Few lessons made sense at the time and, thus, did not sink in. When repackaged years later, executives vigorously enjoyed the rediscovery process. The previously overlooked became sage wisdom. Knowledge they were not ready to receive before became crystal clear in later times.

Pressures continue and accelerate for companies to stay in operation, become competitive, keep ahead of the marketplace and perform quality work. Businesses of all sizes are besieged with opportunities, competing information sources and large amounts of uncertainty. Executives are not really prepared to handle challenges of the moment...much less to begin developing Big Picture thinking.

Seasoned executives face burnout daily. Much of the workforce is in transition...with unclear anchoring of where they've been and where they could head. Young and mid-level workers do not really know what it takes to succeed long-term and are, for the most part, impaired from optimum achievement.

Small and emerging companies, in these troubled times, do not know where to begin. The plethora of seminars, training and writings do not emphasize Big Picture thinking. This comprehensive resource book series opens up the mind and heart of companies...pinpointing what it takes to make it.

The *High Cost of Doing Nothing* analyzes the parts-components of a successful company, how each interplays and the role which Visioning and Strategic Planning play with each branch (business unit). Also detailed are stages in the evolution of a business, leadership development, mentoring and creative ways of retreading old knowledge to enable executives to master change, rather than feel as they're victims of it. Benefits of the book include:

1. Understanding how and why The Business Tree™ (any organization) is standing and growing...instead of looking at each leaf, twig or branch.

2. Inspiring executives to think wholistically about each component of the business in terms of the Big Picture, master change and take companies to new tiers.

3. Fresh approaches toward re-applying past knowledge and experiences. These become Lessons Learned But Not Soon Forgotten.

4. Strategies to reduce *The High Cost of Doing Nothing*™ ...making business more creative, effective and profitable.

About the Author

Hank Moore is that rare one in a million business advisor, a Big Picture Corporate Strategist™, with original, cutting-edge ideas for creating, implementing and sustaining corporate growth throughout every sector of the organization. His Business Tree™ is a trademarked approach to growing, strengthening and evolving business, while mastering change.

He is president of Management Resource Institute, providing Big Picture concepting-planning, visioning, independent company assessments and performance reviews and serves as advisor at the board, CEO and on executive committee levels. Mr. Moore has provided senior level advising services for more than 2,000 client organizations of all sizes (including 90 of the Fortune 500), companies in transition (startup, re-engineering, mergers, going public), public sector entities, professional associations, non-profit organizations and others.

He has published 300+ articles and monographs in

business publications, journals and consumer magazines. Eighteen workbooks of his materials and audio cassette albums are compiled for workshop attendees and corporate clients.

Hank Moore has been accorded 200+ awards for client work and community stewardship, plus citations of merit from five U.S. Presidents, the United Nations, and non-profit councils.

1

Steps Toward Building Better Business

Remediating High Costs by Painting a Big Picture

Potentiality of organizations is a progressive journey from information to insight. Foolhardiness is being righteous about things at the wrong times. People and organizations spend disproportionate amounts of time trying to be or look like someone else...or what they think others look like. Until one becomes one's own best, the futile trail continues.

It takes more courage to pursue a compromise than to pursue an extremist position. Conciliation and reason must be pursued. The skill with which they are approached often spells the difference between total success and political suicide.

People spend so much time relating to and craving the past...or what they think it was. They go to great lengths to recreate the past and devote their lives to avoiding and fighting change.

People take risks to pursue forbidden things. But

what risks will they take to pursue the truth? People believe lies and gossip faster than they believe the truth.

The reality is that individuals and organizations have changed and adapted more than they think. Standing still means moving backward...thus, the subject of this business book.

If they would move forward with their lives, the past would reflect new knowledge. Today is more vivid in people's minds than the past. Today reflects past changes. Tomorrow represents the opportunity to live the kind of life that you want, be the person you have been preparing to be, and become the kind of organization that is successful, rather than dwelling upon past failures and shortcomings.

Mathematical formula: Take what you don't want to believe. Add what you have to believe. You come up with amazing answers.

Expect the best, but prepare for the worst. There is no plan that is fool-proof. Fight for and with the truth. Truth is not always easy to recognize and not always pretty.

In 1920, Warren G. Harding was elected President of the United States on the platform, "Return to Normalcy." There is no such thing as normalcy. The public wants it and tries to create it anyway.

Things are never simple for one who must make decisions and policies. Many factors must be weighed. One cannot always go the path that seems clearest. One who thinks differently and creatively will face opposition. With success of the concept, it gets embraced by others, who claim to have been visionary all along. Shepherding good ideas and concepts does not get many external plaudits. The feeling of accomplishment must be internal. That is a true mark of wisdom.

A great mentor, teacher and role model need not be from the same strata as those whom he-she inspires. Top executives must set standards that others aspire to...including themselves.

People and companies which prefer substance exhibit it by exceeding all standards. Set and meet realistic benchmarks for success. Approach change as an opportunity. Continue asking for feedback. Regularly update policies and procedures. Employ a "futurist" mentality.

Success and failure...it is a matter of perspectives. Out of every 10 transactions in our lives, five will be unqualified successes. One will be a failure. Two will depend upon the circumstances. If approached responsibly, they will become successful. If approached irresponsibly, they will turn into failures. Two will either be successful or will fail, based strictly upon the person's attitude.

A 90% success rate for a person with a good attitude and responsible behavior is an unbeatable percentage. There is no such thing as perfection. Continuous quality improvement means that we benchmark accomplishments and set the next reach a little further.

Success is easily attainable. So, why do people psyche themselves into failing more often they have to...especially when they succeed much more often than they give themselves credit for?

Special dedications to my wife (April), my sisters (Janie and Julie) and my grandchildren (Courtney, Henry, Austin, Tad, Tommy and Erin).

Professional acknowledgments to friends and colleagues whom I wish to salute in this book include Betty Beene, Peter Bijur, Hector DeLeon, Tom Gillis, Lee Iacocca, Lady Bird Johnson, Herb Kelleher, Pat

Kiley, J.W. Marriott, Tom Peters, Carter Rochelle, Larry Sachnowitz, Peter Senge, Bill Spitz, Jon Taylor and Dottie Walters.

It is a rare exaltation to have a dream take shape in your hands. When that moment comes, treasure it and share it. If one cannot invent, one must at least improve upon what they have been given or have to work with.

The rules have changed...always have and always will. The best part about being older is you're not scared very much anymore. The little pictures -- the mosaics -- make up The Big Picture.

A spotlight in the darkness focuses upon whatever is moving. Everything else is blurred in the darkness.

2

The Path from Pleasure to Success

Stages in the Evolution of a Business A Primer on Change Management

Every business, company or organization goes through cycles in its life. At any point, each program or business unit is in a different phase from others. The astute organization assesses the status of each program and orients its team members to meet constant changes and fluctuations.

Strategic Planning facilitates disciplined thinking about the organization, its environment and its future. It identifies conflicts, reinforces team building and serves as a vehicle for monitoring organizational progress.

The planning process is then translated into a company Vision. With that Vision, the organization will evolve steadily toward success. Without any kind of Vision, management will continually apply corrective techniques ("band-aid surgery"), while the company stumbles and falls. The price tag for false surgery is six times that of front-end Vision...a concept that I call The High Cost of Doing Nothing™ (addressed further in Chapter 2).

I've talked with many entrepreneurs and founders of companies which rapidly grew from the seed of an idea they had. Most admitted enjoying the founding phase but lost interest shortly after giving birth. Over and over, they said, "When it stops being fun, I move on. "

After the initial honeymoon, you speak with them and hear rumblings like, "It isn't supposed to be this hard. Whatever happened to the old days? I'm ready to move on. This seems too much like running a business. I'm an idea person, and all this administrative stuff is a waste of my time. I should move on to other new projects."

When they come to me, they want the business to transition smoothly and still make the founders some money. They ask, "Are you the one who comes in here and makes this into a real business?"

I reply, "No. After the caretakers come in and apply the wrong approaches to making something of your business, I'm the one who cleans up after them and starts the business over again." The reality is that I'm even better on the front end, helping business owners avoid the costly pitfalls attached to their losing interest and abdicating to the wrong people.

Most companies enjoy the early stage of success and wish things would stay as in the beginning. When "the fun ends," the hard work begins.

To "go the distance," the organization must complete all seven stages of evolution. There are no fast-forward buttons or skipping steps in developing an effective organization, just as there are no shortcuts in formulating a career and Body of Work.

Stages in the Evolution of a Business

1. Transient Pleasure. Company founders are basking in the glow of initial achievements. There exists an excitement over mission and expertise, as they believe them to be. The founders' creative instincts are satisfied. Egos are inflated.

   In the first year or two, the character of the organization has not changed yet. It reflects what they started with and the first wave of people coming into it. Unfortunately, the founders also brought along the excess baggage of the previous corporate cultures in which they worked. They don't want to be like company X, but, in swinging the pendulum in the opposite direction, they are more like the old company than they realize.

   In the beginning, the founder projects his-her vision into others in the founding team. There is an exchange of egotisms from one person to the other. Pleasures are plentiful in the beginning because great responsibilities are to follow.

2. Big Letdown. The machinery of the company must now perform on its own. Imperfections start to reveal themselves, accompanied by dissatisfactions and the inevitable blaming of others for mistakes. The reality is that no fully

compatible organization exists to handle growth at this point. Founders clingingly wish to return to the early moments of success, or at least the perceptions of victory.

3. Crisis. Principals recognize the end of the early illusions. Now, it's time to become more mature as an organization. Players must now determine if they are willing to make more sacrifices in order to go the distance.

   If management is willing to "stick it out," many strengths and an organizational character will soon be revealed. Founders must reaffirm their commitment toward themselves, the organization and the quest. They start seeing the company (mainly its people) as resources to be cultivated, not exploited.

4. Pain. Some prefer to bask in and try to relive the early experiences, not the current character of the organization that seems to be emerging. It's not fun anymore.

   Now come the "band-aid surgery" approaches that plague otherwise clear thinking. Management begins taking wrong courses of action. Certainly, "trial and error" is admirable and to be expected. Band-aid surgeons usually pursue surface remedies for the pain.

   Many people want quick, easy, flashy fixes without doing the things necessary to maintain staying power. Thus, they move from venture to venture. The realities of doing business for the longterm have now set in.

5. Semi-Permanent Joy. Until they feel the pain and take steps to get through it, the organization will remain stuck. Those who think they are immune to pain and will remain in the pleasure mode are doomed to longterm failure...a fatal flaw of corporate thinking.

   After enduring the crisis and realizing the extent of the pain, rational managers start to see the reasons why they went through this process. They achieve the knowledge and understanding that an evolution has just transpired. Effectively treating the pain and learning from it serves to reinforce the will and zest to achieve further.

6. Assuring Future Success. For longterm survival, it is important to give the seeds of creativity, planning and organizational vision enough time and nurturing to sow. Plan to grow the organization. Grow according to the plan. Craft a Vision from the frustrations, mistakes, failures, missed opportunities, short sightedness and self-sabotage.

7. Understanding the Truisms to Navigate Your Journey. Having worked with hundreds of CEOs (as clients, colleagues and friends), I've absorbed many nuggets of gold. Some of these were taught by me to them. Others were reality-based lessons from the marketplace. All

steered them toward courses of success:

- Organizations do not set out to go bad. They just don't "set out" (little or no planning). Thus, they go off course.

- There is a difference between knowing a product-industry and growing a successful business. Understanding all seven components of a successful company is a concept that I call The Business Tree™ .

- Much of the wisdom to succeed lies outside your company. It must be called upon, sooner rather than later.

- Much of the wisdom to succeed lies within. It must be fine-tuned and utilized.

- People under-perform because they are not given sufficient direction, nurturing, standards of accountability, recognition and encouragement to out-distance themselves. That is a concept that I call The Organization Tree™ .

- Anybody can poke holes at an organization. The art-skill is to create programs and systems which do something constructive. That is a concept that I call Three Rights Offset a Wrong.

- Communicate abstract principles in concrete terms.

- The wheel of an organization must always move outward...establishing commonality and communicating with stakeholders.

- Counter balance left-brain precision for details with right-brain insights and creativity. There is a difference between knowing and feeling. The intellect (left brain) draws something to itself. The will-spirit (right brain) reaches out to something that it loves and aspires to do.

- People must continue to develop professionally in order for the business to grow. That is a concept that I call The Learning Tree™ .

- Whenever the mind knows something that is below, it elevates the knowledge.

- When the mind confronts ideas and concepts which are above it, the inclination is to degrade them.

- When the will-spirit covets anything that is below itself, it is degraded. When people and organizations are obsessed with something beneath them (such as money and fame), the whole entity is pulled down.

- When the will has aspirations and visions above it, standards will rise. It is important to have the right kind of heroes and goals because role model status perpetuates throughout life and permeates organizations.

- It is possible for a company and its managers to know much about certain arts and sciences without having the will to pursue them.

- The level of achievement by a company is commensurate to the level and quality of its vision, goals and tactics. The higher its integrity and character, the higher its people must aspire.

- One learns three times more from failures than from successes. The lessons must be reinforced, studied and applied to future planning. That is a concept that I call The Fine Art of Failure.

- Organizations start to crumble when their people quit on each other.

- No organization can operate in a vacuum. Each needs bases of support, community goodwill and collaborative business partners.

- Unhealthy organizations will always "shoot the messenger" when changes and improvements are introduced.

- Healthy organizations absorb all the knowledge and insight they can...embracing change, continuous quality improvement and planned growth. That is a concept that I call It's Almost Tomorrow.™

Truisms of a Healthy Business

There is a difference between knowing a product-industry and growing a successful business. It is possible for a company and its managers to know much about certain arts and sciences without having the will to pursue them.

Organizations do not set out to go bad. They just don't "set out" (little or no planning). Thus, they go off course.

Much of the wisdom to succeed lies within. It must be recognized, fine-tuned and utilized. Much of the wisdom to succeed lies outside your company. It must be called upon, sooner rather than later.

People under-perform because they are not given sufficient direction, nurturing, standards of accountability, recognition and encouragement to out-distance themselves. Organizations start to crumble when their people quit on each other.

Unhealthy organizations will always "shoot the messenger" when change and improvements are introduced. Healthy organizations absorb all the knowledge and insight they can...embracing change, continuous quality improvement and planned growth.

Anybody can poke holes in an organization. The art-skill is to create programs and systems which do something constructive.

The level of achievement by a company is commensurate to the level and quality of its vision, goals and tactics. The higher its integrity and character, the higher its people must aspire.

Steps in the Corrective Action Process

The Corrective Action Process applies to all individuals operating in a business environment, divisions and entire companies. By employing these analytic tasks, problem solving may be turned into a marketplace advantage:

1. Identify customers for your goods or services, measuring their requirements and problems incurred in delivering to the marketplace.

2. Prioritize problems.

3. Assign responsibilities for problem solving.

4. Apply appropriate problem-solving techniques, including checklists, process analysis, charts, diagrams and force field analysis.

5. Turn recommendations into actions.

6. Review progress. Benchmark the accomplishments. Research serves as planning for the next project phase.

7. Analyze accomplishments in terms of overall organizational Vision and implications for successful achievement of longterm company objectives.

How Companies Develop Staying Power

- Stick around by Default. Some companies are

One Hit Wonders. They have limited utility and don't have what it takes to go the distance. They live short lives because that's all they've got in them. Some One Hit Wonders stay around a little longer than they should have, not because they are doing things right but because they have just stuck around.

- Needed for a Particular Niche. These companies don't try to be all things to all people. They have a specialized market.

- Show Promise to Develop into a Longevity Company. These firms made an effort to justify their niche, not just to fill it by default. They take pride in being the best in their area of expertise and they do business with other quality-oriented companies.

- Time Tested Products, Processes. They are good and plan to get better.

- Willing to Do Things Necessary for Growth. Products and processes only represent one-third of a company's picture. Growth companies take risks and address the other two-thirds on a regular, systematic basis.

- Earned Respect to Continue in Business. Dare to innovate. These companies have a commitment to continuous quality improvement. They also look outward, rather than focusing all resources internally. They view their products, processes and people as a wholistic organization.

- Contributions Beyond the Bottom Line. Understand other reasons for being in business than just the dollars. Make healthy profits, while creating the best products, being a learning organization, setting-upholding standards and continuing to justify leadership position.

Levels of Standards, Ethics

- In order to progress and successfully navigate through the pains, changes and remedies, every organization has to develop its core values and a corporate culture. Though not a part of the initial pleasure phase, having standards and ethics will navigate the journey to success more forceful and surely. Here are seven progressive levels of standards and ethics:

- Base Level. Just needing and attempting to get by. Basics of food, clothing and shelter. Knowing right from wrong. Trying to pursue a good life and aspire to something higher.

- Lowest Common Denominators. Although knowing better, subscribing to prevailing philosophies and behaviors of others. This leads some to take advantage of the system, want more than one's share and fail to be accountable. Sadly, the common denominators are below what they used to be, and society continues to lower them. The mission of a successful person or organization is not to succumb quite that low.

  Lessons from the School of Hard Knocks.

Learning by experiences, trial and error, successes, life skills. Becoming more familiar with one's strengths, weaknesses, opportunities and threats. Understanding what an organization can and cannot accomplish, represent and become. Maximizing one's resources to the most practical advantage.

- Launching a Quest. Striving to learn more and go further. Includes intellectual pursuits, professional realities, nurturing of people skills and executive abilities. At this point, people change careers, and organizations revisit their goals and crystallize new visions.

- Standards. Set and respect boundaries. Many times, people and organizations will attempt to violate those standards or fail to acknowledge their existence. The test is how consistently one sets, modifies and observes one's own standards.

- Values and Vision. No person or organization stands still. It is not enough to accept change but more importantly to benefit from it. It is not enough to see yourself on a higher plateau and quest for more. Success comes from charting a course, encompassing value systems and methodically reaching goals.

- Code of Ethics. Fundamental canons, rules of practice, professional obligations, accountability-measurability, professional development, integrity, objectivity and independence.

> Commitment to uphold and enforce codes of ethics (yours and those of others) and the ethical responsibilities of members in business.

Change Management

Research shows that change is 90% positive and that individuals and organizations change at the rate of 71% per year.

Change is necessitated by a natural flow of events, stemming from changes already made and realized. Some changes are mandated by others in control, and others are necessitated by circumstances outside your control.

The worst blockages of change come from people who possess the "been there, done that" attitude. 87% of the time, they really haven't. Other preventors include middle managers who can't see the forest for the trees, don't want to see beyond the scope and are proud of it.

Young generations who grow up in the houses of the above group see and emulate the anti-change constituencies. They grow up not knowing any better, clinging to the status quos and acting out their limited scope in the classrooms, in social settings and in their early business careers (until they learn better).

Young people in the business world (up to age 40) tend to want instant results, instant gratification and the success of people their senior who have paid substantial dues. As they learn to benefit from change, they mellow into savvy business executives.

To those who block processes of organizational change, things will pass you by, with or without your efforts. Negative efforts will harm your potential for success. Mastering change sooner rather than later has beneficial effects, with no down side.

Styles and Approaches to Mastering Change

Low-Power	Entrepreneur	Innovator
Maintain the status quo	Carve new opportunities	Create future paths for others
Technical proficiency, skills	Develop to an art	Create new modules
Caution Don't rock the boat; Low-profile	Take bold steps to lead and create new things	Courage of convictions, ideologies
Dependency	Autonomy	Self-reliant
Survival	Risk and expansion	Vision, philosophy, future of the business
Bureaucracy	Customer orientation	Leading-championing the marketplace
Fulfill tasks, schedules	Honor-exceed commitments	Provide value-added
Live and let live	Our corner of the world	The global village
Learning	Knowledge	Wisdom

Reasons to Embrace Change and Benefits Provided

People make voluntary and necessary changes everyday. Those who have learned to benefit from change retain a profound commitment to the process, reaping the benefits of continually changing opportunities.

The steps toward mastering change include:

1. Recognizing what has already occurred.

2. Perceiving new areas of change.

3. Prioritizing the work to be done.

4. Changing gradually and gracefully.

5. Behavior modification.

6. Quality management and orientation.

7. Commitment to furthering, monitoring, advocating and inspiring change.

To realize full benefits from change, be real with yourself about the changes. Confront what has been done to sabotage success. Be willing to make changes. Benchmark the changes.

Be accountable for fallout, by-products and after-effects of change. Advocate future changes...to yourself and others. Continually re-enact this process with other change management opportunities.

Changing with successful results beats the alternative. Organizations and professionals who become stuck in ruts and stubbornly cling to the past are dinosaurs, whom the marketplace will pass by.

Research shows that change is 90% beneficial. So why do people fight what's in their best interest? Change management is an art, not a death sentence.

Professionals, specialists and technicians owe their careers and livelihoods to change. Because they are educated and experienced at new techniques, they have market power.

Change is not as high-risk as some people fear. Failure to change costs the company six times more. Lost business, opportunity costs and product failures are signs of neglect, poor management, failure to plan-anticipate and grow the company.

Those who champion change will positively advance their companies and careers. It accelerates the learning curve and success ratio. Those who do not get on the bandwagon will not last in the company. Those who excel develop leadership skills, empowered teams and efficiencies.

Leaders who expose their teams to new territories help them see how they adapt within that framework. Championing change can mark the next tier in an executive's development.

A well-intentioned person may want and try so hard to do the right thing that he-she makes mistakes and ultimately does the wrong thing. It is the mark of a great person to admit mistakes, correct the course and move on. Another mark of a great leader is to let his people lead too...and give them the reins to do so effectively.

Change helps you do business in the present and helps plan for the future. Without mastering the challenges of a changing world, companies will not be optimally successful.

The company-organization which manages change remains successful, ahead of the competition and is a business-industry leader. Meanwhile, other companies will have become victims of change because they stood by and did nothing.

3

The Doing Nothing Syndrome

Each year, one-third of the U.S. Gross National Product goes toward cleaning up problems, damages and otherwise high costs of doing either nothing or doing the wrong things.

On the average, it costs six times the investment of preventive strategies to correct business problems (compounded per annum and exponentially increasing each year). In some industries, the figure is as high as 30 times...six is the mean average.

The old adage says: "An ounce of prevention is worth a pound of cure." One pound equals 16 ounces. In that scenario, one pound of cure is 16 times more costly than an ounce of prevention.

Human beings, as we are, never do everything perfectly on the front end. There always must exist a learning curve. Research shows that we learn three times more from failures than from successes. The mark of a quality organization is how it corrects mistakes and prevents them from recurring.

Running a profitable and efficient organization means effectively remediating damage before it accrues. Processes and methodologies for researching, planning, executing and benchmarking activities will reduce that pile of costly coins from stacking up.

Doing nothing becomes a way of life. It's amazing how many individuals and companies live with their heads in the sand. Never mind planning for tomorrow...we'll just deal with problems as they occur. This mindset, of course, invites and tends to multiply trouble.

There are seven costly categories of doing nothing, doing far too little or doing the wrong things in business:

1. Cleaning Up Problems: Waste, Spoilage. Poor controls. Down-time. Lack of employee motivation and activity. Back orders because they were not properly stocked. Supervisory involvement in retracing problems and effecting solutions.

2. Rework: Product recalls. Make-good for shoddy or inferior work. Poor location. Regulatory red tape. Excess overhead.

3. Missed Marks: Poor controls on quality. Fallout damage from employees with problems (For example, a substance abuser negatively impacts 20 people before treatment is applied.) Undercapitalization. Unsuccessful marketing. Unprofitable pricing.

4. Damage Control: Crisis management. Lawsuits

incurred because procedures were not upheld. Affirmative action violations. Violations of OSHA, ADA, EEOC, EPA and other codes. Disasters due to employee carelessness, safety violations, oversights, etc. Factors outside your company that still impede your ability to do business.

5. Recovery and Restoration: Repairing ethically wrong actions. Empty activities. Mandated cleanups, corrections and adaptations. Employee turnover, rehiring and retraining. Isolated or unrealistic management. Bad advice from the wrong consultants. Repairing a damaged company's reputation.

6. Retooling and Restarting: Mis-use of company resources, notably its people. Converting to existing codes and standards. Chasing the wrong leads, prospects or markets. Damage caused by inertia or lack of progress. The anti-change "business as usual" philosophy. Long-term expenses incurred by adopting quick fixes.

7. Opportunity Costs: Failure to understand what business they're really in. Inability to read the warning signs or understand external influences. Failure to change. Inability to plan. Over-dependence upon one product or service line. Diversifying beyond the scope of company expertise. Lack of an articulated, well-implemented vision.

7 Primary Factors of The High Cost of Doing Nothing™

1. Failure to value and optimize true company resources.
2. Poor premises, policies, processes, procedures, precedents and planning.
3. Opportunities not heeded or capitalized.
4. The wrong people in the wrong jobs. Under-trained employees.
5. The wrong consultants (miscast, untrained, improperly used).
6. Lack of articulated focus and vision. With no plan, no journey will be completed.
7. Lack of movement really means falling behind the pack and eventually losing ground.

What Could Have Reduced These High Costs:

1. Effective policies and procedures.
2. Setting and respecting boundaries.
3. Realistic expectations and measurements.
4. Training and development of people.

5. Commitments to quality at all links in the chain.

6. Planning.

7. Organizational vision.

"They can't hang you for saying nothing," quipped President Calvin Coolidge in the 1920's. He spent more time doing chores at his farm and taking long naps than taking care of the nation's business. Coolidge prided himself upon doing little and, thus, failed to see crises brewing during his presidency. This "keep your head in the sand" mentality is prevalent of people who move on and let others clean up the damage.

High Cost Case Studies ...Doing Nothing and Doing the Wrong Things.

The Titanic

One of the greatest tragedies in history, the sinking of the Titanic, can be attributed to carelessness, insufficient planning and stubborn pride.

People literally went down with the ship while still quoting the ship's marketing hype, "Everybody knows this ship cannot sink." They really believed the spin and rationalized it as a false hope to avert disaster. They were so sure that tragedy could not happen to them, believed themselves to be invincible, had false senses of security and exhibited unnecessarily stoical behavior when confronted with the harsh realities of death.

In 1912, the Titanic, a Trans-Atlantic ship on its maiden voyage, hit an iceberg and sank. Though some people escaped by life boats, there were still 1,502 people killed.

If any of these had occurred, chances are that every life would have been saved. The Titanic would not have sunk if **any** of these precautions-actions had occurred:

- Management...had the ship's officers heeded one of the six iceberg warnings.
- Planning...had the ship's design required better lighting to see a potential collision.
- Timing...had the ship hit the iceberg 15 seconds sooner or 13 seconds later.
- Planning...had the water tight bulkheads been one deck higher.
- Supplies...if the ship had carried enough life boats.
- Regulations...had the distress signal to a nearby ship been heeded and acted upon.

Not only did the people die, but it was the end of an era in travel. Credibility toward steamships was shaken. Safety became more important in the luxury travel industry. Other forms of travel could serve customers better, faster and cheaper. Concern for corporate savings at the expense of quality was raised.

Think of other disasters that brought similar

concerns home and forced major changes in planning, policy, safety, implementation and accountability: (1) Fires and collapses in commercial buildings, due to use of sub-standard materials or improper safety precautions. (2) Citizen outcries over prejudice, hate and bigotry actions by people in charge. (3) Unnecessary duplication of services by public sector and non-profit entities. (4) Chemical plant explosions. (5) Improper discharge of substances into the ozone. (6) Maneuvers, where improper planning cost property and lives. (7) Insensitivity of organizations to their customers.

Learning from History

The basic cause of World War II was a failure to uphold the peace treaty following World War I. Countries let circumstances fester (notably the Hitler regime) that paying attention to and adhering to the peace treaty would have precluded.

Throughout the 1920s, the U.S. spent $50 million per year in trying vainly to enforce the highly unpopular Prohibition Act. Bootleggers, racketeers and mobsters made billions of dollars and established footholds in territories that were impossible to retract. An unpopular law spearheaded by a zealous few was never really enforced, and its criminal perpetrators became "folk heroes" to many.

People at Work

The current success rate for organizational hires is 14%. If further research is put into looking at the total person and truly fitting the person to the job, then the success rate soars to 75%. That involves testing and more sophisticated hiring practices.

Retaining good employees, involving training, motivation and incentives, is yet another matter.

According to research conducted by the Ethics Resource Center:

- Employees of organizations steal 10 times more than do shoplifters.

- Employee theft and shoplifting account for 15% of the retail cost of merchandise.

- 35% of employees steal from the company.

- 28% of those who steal think that they deserve what they take.

- 21% of those who steal think that the boss can afford the losses.

- 56% of employees lie to supervisors.

- 41% of employees falsify records and reports.

- 31% of the workforce abuses substances.

One out of every 20 employees has substance or alcohol abuse problems with resulting behaviors which in turn adversely effect another 20 people in their lives. Employees with substance abuse problems cost their companies $7,000 per year in downtime or lost days, $9,500 in make-good and work redo and another $15,000 in opportunity and credibility costs to the organization. Companies with good Employee Assistance Programs reduce these high costs and retain the services of valuable workers.

Careless actions by a construction worker caused irreparable damage to New York City's oldest synagogue. Mishandling of a blow torch ignited a blaze that required 250 firefighters to contain. Congregation members were displaced, and the rebuilding took another year.

Public Sector Actions and Misactions

An outsourced prison management firm was charged with unnecessary violence against inmates in a Texas prison. Films of brutal beatings and unleashed dogs on the prisoners made the national news. The State of Missouri cancelled its contract with the State of Texas. Other states began investigating how their monies were spent in outsourcing prison management. The actions of one contractor put the concept of privatized law enforcement under question.

The former chief of the Texas Department of Criminal Justice was indicted on six counts of conspiracy, bribery, money laundering and other charges stemming from a meat contract to feed prisoners. Changes included the payment of a $20,000 incentive by the food company to get a $33.6 million contract to sell to the state. Meat company officials were also indicted.

The Mars rover program was a great interest and spawned renewed curiosity in space exploration.

When the camera got stalled and could not send back pictures, public attention quickly evaporated. After other frustrating incidents with equipment failure and downtime, the project was scrubbed. It was revealed that $290 billion of taxpayer dollars were wasted because small communications errors went undetected. NASA sacrificed a few mid-management executives for the errors in communications and quality control.

At a university campus, 200 cases of food poisoning were reported. Hospitalized students made the news. The university spent time and resources on damage control and investigation, with the possibilities of litigation and decreased development support in mind. Alas, it was determined that one employee failed to wash his hands and transmitted bacteria into the food that was consumed by the 200 students and then some. The employee failed to obey the university's health code.

Special prosecutor Kenneth Starr's office spent five years and more than $60 million taxpayer dollars engaging in what many considered to be political pursuits. Of that, $5 million was spent on the Monica Lewinsky investigation by itself. The news media reaped audience numbers and percentage points from gossip, allegations and public fascination associated with the investigations.

A city council was fined $150,000, based upon the over-zealousness of one council member. Her efforts to set limits against multi-family dwelling construction were found to deny the right by one builder to do business. The court ruling said the builder was unfairly denied right to the marketplace due to prejudicial specifications.

When heavy flooding occurs, residents are forced to evacuate and are charged with millions of dollars to repair property. Property owner groups charge county flood control districts with responsibility. Their public outcries and class action suits charge that sufficient planning could have averted much of the damage.

Gtech Corporation of Rhode Island, which runs the Texas Lottery, recently paid $725,000 to the Lottery's former director to settle a lawsuit which she had filed against them. This was an out-of-court settlement for the former director losing her $90,000 per year job. Allegedly, Gtech had paid the director's former boyfriend in order to have leverage over her position. This controversy broke after Gtech's former national sales manager was convicted of federal kickback violations in New Jersey. Former Texas Lieutenant Governor Ben Barnes was dismissed as a $3 million per year lobbyist for Gtech but was given a $23 million severance by the company.

Credibility of the F.B.I. was questioned after incidents of insufficient or improper handling of scientific evidence surfaced. The once unshakable reputation of the Bureau has been rigorously put under a microscope, in light of trials resulting from the bombing of the Oklahoma City Federal Building, the Houston City Hall Sting and other courtroom proceedings.

A recent audit of a county hospital district stated that more than $20 million has been spent over five years on a computer contract that is so vague and poorly monitored that county auditors say it cost taxpayers hundreds of thousands of dollars.

A Titan IV-A rocket exploded August 12, 1998,

over Cape Canaveral, FL.

The nation lost $1.3 billion in space equipment, including a spy satellite. This disaster cost each U.S. taxpayer $11. The previous Titan explosions, in 1993 and 1986 at Vandenberg Air Force Base in California, have been traced to failures in the casings of the solid rocket boosters, made by United Technologies in San Jose, CA.

Medicare lost about 7.1 cents of every dollar to fraud, wastes and mistakes last year. Based upon the dollar value of sample bills, auditors estimated that Medicare paid out $12.6 billion more than it should have. That's 7.1% of the total $176.1 billion that Medicare paid directly to health care providers, including doctors and hospitals.

The 1999 trial and conviction for a racist killing in Jasper, Texas, put a strain on that tiny town's treasury.

To pay the $500,000 costs for justice being reached, the State of Texas contributed $100,000, and every Jasper resident was assessed an increase in property taxes by $40 per year.

It costs $55 per day to house prison inmates. Additional costs are $177 to overhead expenses. The average lethal injection costs $1 million, counting the costs for arrest, investigations, lawyers, trials, appeals and all other actions before the convicted felon is executed.

During 1999 bombings in Yugoslavia, a misdirected mission caused the accidental bombing of a Chinese embassy.

To make amends, the U.S. government paid $4.5 million for the rebuilding of the destroyed structure.

Corporate Actions

When the federal government sued IBM for antitrust violation, in 1972, the process dragged on 13 years and cost both sides hundreds of millions of dollars. Joint federal-state antitrust actions against Microsoft promise to be equally costly to both sides.

The Exxon Valdez oil spill in Alaska cost millions to clean up. Worse, it put most oil companies under a cloud of public distrust. Some companies spent large sums of money in proclaiming their points of difference. Others simply did nothing and continued business as usual. Handling of other oil disasters is continually compared to the Valdez, as the benchmark. Public confidence in energy firms has been shaken ever since the Valdez incident.

Union Pacific Railroad and Southern Pacific Railroad merged. The promise, like most mergers, was greater operating efficiency. Predictably, cost-cutting measures were enacted. Service decayed, complicated by several derailments. The gridlock stunted service, costing customers millions of dollars. At one point, shipments were backed up as much as 30 days. Investigations showed that it would take up to five years to get service back to where it was before the merger.

The National Transportation Safety Board blamed failures by ValuJet Airlines, its SabreTech maintenance contractor and federal officials as "probable causes" of the 1996 crash that killed 110. "The ValuJet accident resulted from failures up and down the line," stated NTSB Chairman James Hall. "The chain of events here led all the way from the regulators to the executive board to the workroom at

SabreTech. Here it seems the entire system that is there to protect the public failed." Dozens of lawsuits followed these revelations.

In 1997, Boeing Corporation had more business than they could handle. One year later, with more than $80 billion in back orders, the company was forced to downsize, cutting 48,000 jobs.

A study was conducted concerning the economic impact of new stadiums and sports franchises upon major city economies. The conventional wisdom, of course, is that such things are good for local economies—the bars, hotels, transporters, peanut vendors, etc. all get a piece of the action. The study found, though, that in the great majority of cases, there was little if any economic benefit once all things were considered: community division, costs of promoting, financing, construction, damage control, etc.

An abandoned paint factory was deemed to be a severe environmental hazard, due to emissions and its effect on the neighboring water supply. The owners had been previously cited by the Environmental Protection Agency but eluded without being arrested. It cost the EPA $1.2 million in taxpayer funds to clean up the mounting debacle.

Crimes

In February, 2000, hack attacks on major websites like Ebay and Yahoo cost $1.2 billion. Costs included $1 billion in lost stock values-sales, $100 million in beefing up security and $100 million in lost business.

31% of young people imprisoned for crime said that they imitated acts seen on television and in the movies.

Costs of Strikes

The 1997 strike by United Parcel Service workers left a mark on customers—$50 million in lost business. The 15-day strike adversely affected some customers on a long-term basis. Total costs of the strike: $100 million.

The 1998 strikes against General Motors cost the company more than $50 million. Workers lost wages, production was delayed and the marketplace suffered.

Costs of other high-profile strikes (to customers and to the economy): 1997 British Airways strike, $200 million.

Domino Effects, Costly Mistakes

The Mars Orbiter weather satellite, which cost the taxpayers $125 million exploded. One team of designers at Lockheed Martin put the command instructions in English and another in the metric system. Conversions of the two calculations to each other were not made. Nobody in the company's or NASA's quality control chain caught the programming mistake. The orbiter missed its target, exploded and created expensive "toast." Questions about privatizing space agency functions were loudly raised in the media, public discussion and Congress.

Radioactive materials were not treated properly in Japan, causing widespread contamination. Instead of following proper procedures of mixing, storage and settling of radioactive materials, workers took short cuts by mixing materials in a bucket. This 1999 incident was termed the second worst radioactive disaster, after 1983's Chernobyl.

A power failure struck San Francisco, California, at the height of the rush hour on December 8, 1998. It cut service to more than one million people, leaving train commuters stranded under San Francisco Bay, stalling electric buses in the streets and forcing businesses, some schools and the stock exchange to shut down. This disaster resulted in the death of a 75-year-old woman who was crossing the street. Hundreds were trapped in elevators. Hospitals canceled elective surgeries. Most computer-effected operations were shut down.

It happened because a construction crew at a transmission station in San Mateo County forgot to remove the ground wire after completing maintenance on a substation switchboard, causing a blowout and triggering a chain reaction that knocked two generators off-line. Human error was blamed. Cost of this "human error" to the San Francisco economy was in millions of dollars and lost productivity hours.

A handful of band members from two rival universities got into a skirmish on the football field, resulting in suspensions from the conference and negative publicity. Both schools had to take expensive and time-consuming steps to apologize, show remorse and save face, all stemming from poor behavioral choices by a few students.

In Cincinnati, Ohio, a white police officer shot an unarmed black youth. Public outcry from this incident resulted in protests and looting of property. The town was put under curfew, and national attention focused upon racial division, profiling and other profound problems that had gone untreated in the city. High costs of property loss, violence and repairs to the city's image were a result of diversity issues that could have and should have been addressed positively long ago.

Public Curiosities

The O.J. Simpson trial was an international curiosity. It was a bonanza for gossip mongers and spoke to the addictions of the public for escapism entertainment fare.

The Clinton Crisis

Had Bill Clinton taken different actions at one of these points, his investigation would not have escalated:

(1) Made a full admission in the Gennifer Flowers case.

(2) Offered a settlement to Paula Jones.

(3) Made a concession to Linda Tripp. (Her outrage at the President's lawyer saying that she was not to be believed resulted in Tripp taping conversations and turning evidence over to Kenneth Starr's office.)

(4) Refrained from attempts to cover up the Monica Lewinsky case.

(5) Been more candid about the affair in January, 1998.

(6) Offered a stronger apology after testifying to the grand jury in August, 1998.

(7) Attempted to work with Congress earlier to avoid the matter going to an impeachment.

Things Business Does Not Address Until Costs Pile Up

Accountabilities
Habits
Processes
Actions
Learning curve
Quality control
Assumptions
Operations
Research
Attitudes
Opportunities
Rumors
Consequences
Outcomes
Skills
Corrections
People
Strengths
Egos
Policies
Successes
Erroneous information
Problems
Threats
Getting informed advice
Procedures
Weaknesses

More Things Business Does Not Address Until Costs Pile Up

Levels of Doing Things:

1. Partial or Distorted
2. Not Well Thought Out
3. Popular or Politically Correct
4. The Only Recourse
5. The Right Thing to Do
6. Correct and Accurate
7. The Best Thing to Do

Motivations for Doing Things:

1. Do by Direction
2. Do by Default. Things done because it was the only choice
3. Need to
4. Want to
5. In our best interest to do so
6. Should, would and could do

7. Committed, energized and eager to do or achieve

Levels of Doing The Wrong Things:

1. Actions-Inactions
2. Wrong, Inaccurate and Biased Information
3. Inappropriate Choices and Judgments
4. Poor Timing-Response
5. People Skills Flaws
6. Coverups, Denial and Scapegoating
7. Fighting Change

The High Cost of Not Listening to Advice:

1. Bad Advice
2. Wrong Advice
3. Buying Someone's Bill of Goods
4. Doing What Will Spin Well
5. Actions That Get Artificial Results
6. Perpetuates the Cycle of Management by Crisis
7. Longterm Irrecoverable Costs

4

The Doing Nothing Tree

100 Reasons Why Good Businesses Go Bad

Failure to take pro-active business strategies and steps becomes a habit in any organization. Let one thing slide and another layer of problems will appear. It's easier and more comfortable to look the other way.

Organizations try to maintain the status quo, thinking it to be their best course, by finding greater comfort with the "same old, same old," rather than new concepts. Habits become anointed as "traditions" by the organizations denying the implications of change, hoping their problems will go away and focusing anywhere besides their own culpability with problems. Problems are seemingly swept under the carpet by blaming mistakes away, refusal to take personal accountability and failure to emphasize the positives.

There are costs attached to neglect, indecision and non-actions. Failure to take pro-active measures costs the organization exponentially each year by six.

You and your company will pay the bills for damage caused by inertia or lack of progress. Waste, spoilage, down-time and empty activities currently existing bring down productivity and profitability potential.

Lack of having a cohesive marketplace strategy means you're chasing too many of the wrong leads, prospects or markets, which sets the company back.

By sticking to "business as usual," even when it is clearly not what it used to be, companies began telling themselves the great lies which justify their refusal to change and believe them to be truisms.

Long-term expenses incurred by adopting quick fixes and applying "band-aid surgery" to problems usually result in opening new ones. Possessing an inability to spot where the current and upcoming opportunities lie result in the company abdicating its marketplace to others. The company falls behind the competition...out of failure to change, grow and succeed, plus failure to recognize and reward the strengths within your own organization.

7 Levels of Handling Problems...determining the effectiveness of solutions

1. Do Nothing. Think that things will work themselves out or that causes of problems will go away. Research shows that doing nothing results in creating 3-6 more affiliated problems.

2. Deny, Actively Avoid. Don't see problems as such. Keep one's head in the sand and remain impervious to warning signs of trouble. Go to

great lengths to put positive spins on anything that may point back to one's self, department or organization as being problematic.

3. Cover Up. Coverups cost 6-12 times that of addressing problems upfront. In addition to financial, coverup costs can include the effects upon morale, activity levels, productivity, decision making, creativity, adaptation and innovation. Even after the coverup has fully played out, there is an additional cost: the period of recovery and restoration of confidence.

4. Partially Address. Perform band-aid surgery, at such time as action is demanded. Address signs and symptoms, without addressing root causes. This shows that something is being done, but it is often the wrong thing at the wrong time.

5. Handle in Politically Correct Terms. Some problems are addressed, partially or fully, because bosses, regulators or stakeholders expect it. Some are handled for fear of repercussion. This motive results in tentative actions, with lip service paid to deep solutions.

6. Address Head-On. Problems are, of course, opportunities to take action. Everyone makes mistakes, and success lies in the way that problems are recognized, solved and learned from. The mark of a true manager is to recognize problems sooner, rather than later. The mark of an effective leader is the ability and willingness

to take swift and definitive actions. The mark of an empowered team is its participation in this process. The mark of a successful organization is its endorsement and insistence upon this method of action.

7. Address in Advance, Preparing for Situations. Pro-actively study for patterns. 85% of the time, crises which are predicted, pre-addressed and strategized are averted. The skill in pre-managing problems is a fundamental tenet of a quality-oriented organization.

100 Reasons Why Good Businesses Go Bad

These are the 100 reasons why good organizations of all sizes go astray, categorized per each branch of The Business Tree™ . Take the following test. Grade your company. More than 40 bullet points checked is a failing score. Consider these negatives as opportunities to improve growth and success.

The business you're in

1. Service is rendered, and products are designed-and manufactured the same way in which they always were.

2. Technical abilities and specialties are not further developed after the company's initial successes in creating their widget.

3. The presumption held is that, if it worked for the company founder(s), then it still works for

the rest of the industry and all competitors within it.

4. Management doesn't see the need to use industry consultants or technical specialists.

5. Core business supplier relationships have not been examined or updated lately.

6. No investment has been made toward quality controls.

7. The company applies "band-aid surgery" toward core business issues and problems but only at such a time when they absolutely have to or are forced to.

Running the business

8. The business continues to be run as they always have operated, citing the first way of doing things as a "tradition."

9. Top management subscribes to the philosophy, "If it ain't broke, don't fix it."

10. Lack of formal organizational structure leaves many company executives blamable but not accountable, with many unclear as to their roles and responsibilities.

11. Practices, procedures, operations, structure are not documented in writing, nor are they communicated to employees.

12. Measuring performance is not factored into the production continuum. Management asks, "Why bother to review everything? Let's just do it."

13. The physical plant is not regularly studied, updated or modified. Management contends, "It was good enough when we built it and still fits our needs."

14. Cost containment is the main driver of all process applications, technologies, equipment, supplies and systems.

15. Distribution standards are not documented, practiced or measured.

16. Time management is not observed, studied or utilized. The attitude is perpetuated, "When it's ready, it's ready."

17. The company continues to stockpile inventories. No efforts are made to reduce surplus or adopt practices such as "just in time delivery."

18. Management does not consult the lawyers until the company gets in trouble or is sued.

19. The organization rarely outsources, if ever. The prevailing attitude is: "We have enough engineers and technicians working for us. Why pay others on the outside?"

20. Executives believe that computer software is

the one and only answer to take care of all company problems and that computer consultants are expert business strategists.

21. No telecommunications system or strategy exists. "We already have telephones," they cry, as a rag-tag setup angers customers and diverts business.

22. The administrative function does not have a written, formal purchasing plan. "When we need something, just send out for it."

23. To cut expenses, repair and maintenance contracts are not held and are often not renewed.

24. Equipment is bought outright, rather than leased or financed.

25. Continuous quality improvement is not practiced. No consideration is given toward creating or implementing such a program.

26. The company applies "band-aid surgery" toward process and operations facets...but only at such a time when it absolutely has to or is forced to.

Financial

27. The belief is steadfastly held that every product must make a profit, at all times.

28. Few, if any, profits are plowed back into the

business. Few longterm investments are made.

29. The company's book of assets are not adequately valued or managed.

30. Owners believe that the only reason for being in business is to make as much money for themselves as possible.

31. Cash flow, forecasting and budgeting are inconsistent, if monitored at all.

32. Policies with receivables are not formal, and squeaky wheels get the grease.

33. The business officer does not concern himself about equity and debt financing. The contention is that such things are only applicable to public companies.

34. The company doesn't call or consult the accounting firm until income tax season or audit time.

35. Banking and investing relationships are not fully valued and are perceived as free advice from vendors.

36. Creditor payments are drug out as long as possible...even paying past-due interest when charged. The game is to keep them waiting...using their money interest-free, without realizing the costs of administrative minutia.

37. The company has gotten a reputation for being slow-pay. The accounts payable officer never mediates differences with creditors until they sue, figuring that if one wears creditors down, they will hopefully go away.

38. Finance charges are paid at maximum rates. No attempt has been made to negotiate volume discounts.

39. The company buys the cheapest insurance, which leaves company employees under-covered, unnecessarily bothered by third-party red tape and not as focused on company loyalty as they could be.

40. Management does not see any relationship of benefits packages toward heightened employee productivity.

41. The company applies "band-aid surgery" toward financial dynamics...but only at such time when they absolutely have to or are forced to.

People

42. The corporate culture is slow paced, sluggish and without professionalism.

43. Employees are complacent and rarely carry the company banner forward. Low morale persists and builds upon itself.

44. Human resources does not pay recruiters and personnel firms. They run ads only when they need people to fill specific job titles.

45. Human resources hire only to fill vacant jobs, rather than available and recruitable match talent to potential company opportunities.

46. Top management does not see itself as needing to have people development, skills or team building responsibilities.

47. Human Resources department perceives that it knows what the company is all about and is expected to take care of all problems, without top management intervening.

48. Only executives get bonuses. Others should be grateful to get a regular paycheck.

49. The boss takes the attitude: "Those people work for me. I don't work for them."

50. A regular paycheck is thought to be the only and best incentive for people to work.

51. Upon hiring, employees are handed nebulous job descriptions and are supposed to perform. If they don't, they're fired.

52. Management believes that troublesome employees are easily replaceable and does not realize the economic sense of saving productive workers.

53. Executives see themselves as being the heart of this company. "They do the real work, especially the ones whom the CEO brought on board."

54. The value of training is not understood, appreciated or related to employee performance or the bottom line. They ask, "Why spend money on professional development?"

55. The company develops and teaches all workshops and seminars with in-house talent. The value of outsourced training by niche experts is not comprehended.

56. Management does not know how to discern among or properly utilize business consultants. To cover its lack of analytical ability, it queries, "Why do consultants keep looking at how the organization operates? They cannot possibly know what we know."

57. Performance reviews are arbitrary and are never held with any regularity nor are employees judged against viable corporate objectives.

58. Empowerment, team building and people skills programs are seen as necessary evils and are minimized.

59. The company applies "band-aid surgery" toward people and their issues...but only at such time they absolutely have to or are forced to.

Business development

60. The company does not have a clearly defined image or communications strategy.

61. Branding depends upon the boss' latest whim or whatever company the boss wants to copy.

62. The communications section manager is never in the planning or production loops nor is asked to advise corporate management.

63. No formal, written or measurable sales plan exists. Goals are either unreasonably high or dangerously low.

64. Marketing and sales are viewed as the same thing and, thus, are lumped together in management's consciousness.

65. No formal marketing plan exists. Marketing is done either on a whim or after the fact.

66. The sales force is not valued and is seen as a necessary evil. "If sales slack off, then we fire people and go hire those who can sell."

67. Sales and marketing people are under-trained, under-managed and threatened with termination for not meeting quotas — always with an axe poised over their heads.

68. No formal written advertising program exists.

69. No formal written public relations program exists.

70. Advertising and public relations are viewed as the same thing and, thus, are lumped together in management's consciousness.

71. The cheapest possible promotional activities are utilized. Incentives, advertising specialties and customer appreciation items are not factored into the marketing budget.

72. All creative work is done in-house. No need to buy graphic, audio-visual, advertising, research or other promotional services is seen. Thus, expenses are incurred to fully staff a creative services department.

73. Top management does not see itself as needing to maintain or contribute to Business Development responsibilities.

74. Incorrect assumptions preclude an aggressive communications strategy. "The marketplace knows who we are. Why should we have to adapt?"

75. Marketing and sales are viewed only as necessary evils. Engineers and other core business practitioners disdain the concepts and refuse to cooperate with marketing and sales.

76. The company applies "band-aid surgery" toward business development...but only at such

a time when they absolutely have to or are forced to.

Body of knowledge

77. The company maintains a false sense of success, rarely attributing the contributions of employees and scapegoating others for management's own shortcomings.

78. Critical faculties toward pro-active change become low, and, thus, the company remains stuck in a complacent mode.

79. Management has an inability to predict or stay ahead of trends. "Why worry about changing markets, opportunities, barriers, since we don't need to change?"

80. Decision makers never learn the lessons of failure or the true reasons for successes.

81. The company follows its industry, rather than leading. Product and service development take place after its competitors do the innovating.

82. Management keeps its head in the sand. The rationale is "Nothing that goes on outside our company affects our business in any way."

83. There is an unwillingness to invest in research or to comprehend how it might impact corporate growth.

84. There is a reluctance to joint-venture or work with other companies. Some contend: "They just want to steal our customers."

85. It is believed that government agencies and regulators are to be avoided, feared, fought or ignored. The concept of collaboratively volunteering to work with them in achieving mutual goals is not on the radar.

86. Company leadership feels that it does not owe anything back to the communities in which it works nor has the need to interface with them.

87. The company applies "band-aid surgery" toward anything affecting the wholistic operation of the company but only at such a time when they absolutely have to or are forced to.

The big picture

88. Applying "band-aid surgery" to problems keeps the company from ever having to create, face or benchmark against a Big Picture.

89. No Shared Vision is ever crafted, let alone articulated and followed.

90. Low corporate self-esteem persists.

91. The CEO remains isolated from creative, contrary or augmentive viewpoints. "Why share ideas and philosophies with others? I know what I'm doing." Corporate purges result from isolationism.

92. Creative business practices are not welcome, sought or achieved.

93. Strategic planning is viewed as a superfluous exercise that is only applicable to companies other than ours.

94. Strategic planning is done when the boss goes away for the weekend and comes back with a list of things to be executed by others.

95. The assumption is that one corporate culture is held equally by all employees. "Whatever the company thinks so will all of its employees."

96. "Outside-the-box thinking does not apply to us, nor will be tolerated. What is it anyway?"

97. "We do not engage in unethical practices. What is an ethics statement?"

98. "The quality process means doing things the way we've always done them, without deviation or interference by unwanted intruders. What is Continuous Quality Improvement anyway?"

99. No crisis management, preparedness or prevention program exists. Management deals with each crisis as it comes up.

100. At best, change will be tolerated. Most resources have already been expended to fight and prevent change from occurring.

Tallying the High Costs of Doing Nothing

On a scale of 1-100, how did the company which you rated fare? If the total number of bullets checked exceeds 40, this means assured failure. 20-40 means barely getting by...which is not acceptable in today's competitive economy.

Think of the changes and improvements necessary to get the organization to have less than 20 bullet points checked because that's what it will take to succeed.

Most of the statements quoted above are voiced by poorly run companies which are clueless about sophisticated growth skills. However, pro-active techniques for actualized company growth can be learned. An articulated, well-implemented vision will pre-empt and prevent many of the mistakes that companies make.

There are two choices, completely up to each organization: (1) The company that does not champion change will falter and die. (2) The company that capitalizes upon change (which is 90% beneficial) will grow and prosper.

As each company pursues the strategic planning process, a deeper understanding of the business develops. The company begins to address and master change, rather than becoming a victim of it.

5

100 Biggest Excuses They Use

Euphemisms Most Often Heard—Rationales and Reasons Why Businesses Fail

Some people and organizations go to great extremes to place spins, rationalize or save face in their business lives. Often, they offer sweeping generalizations that involve making far-fetched excuses or scapegoating someone else.

Criticizing others may be cloaked as a subtle or even polite dialog.

Yet, behind these often-voiced expressions lie fallacies in reasoning, the wrong facts, jealousy, animosity, personal self-defeat or cluelessness of the speaker.

When people pose the following questions or statements, there often lurk sarcasm or hidden agendas behind the "seemingly innocent" comments.....

Failing to make investments in future company success:

- I'm building a new house right now. Just took a vacation. Got to send the kid to college (or some other personal reason).

- Can't spend money on marketing my business to customers.

- We just bought a bunch of equipment.

- Well, we do have to pay taxes.

- Have to make cuts everywhere else to pay for rising production costs.

- We make a good product...that should be enough.

- Why must we spend time on things other than our core business?

- We have a good company image. That's enough to sustain us.

- We can dispense with all that employee training and professional development.

- We just cannot afford to make the investments.

Rationalizing organizational setbacks:

- We were growing too fast anyway.

- It was time to pull in our reins and get back to basics.
- We took a risk once, and it didn't work out.
- This hasn't been our lucky year.
- It's a tight economy. When things get better, then we'll expand.
- If we didn't have so much (any) competition, then we would be on Easy Street.
- That was caused by previous management. We blame it on them.
- We're lean and mean now...cut out all the fat.
- Our people just need to work a little harder.
- Those advocate groups did it to us again.
- Economic forces beyond our control are at work.
- But, we're still making money.
- If our people would think more about what they're doing, then we would be successful.

- That's our problem...people thinking but not doing...people doing but not thinking.

Rationalizing poor service or quality:

- You won't get it any better elsewhere. If you don't believe it, go try to find out.
- We're number one in sales.
- Our people were hired to do their jobs. They know what they're doing.
- Nobody has complained about this issue before. The problem must be with you.
- Quality is our middle name.
- We've got the latest technology.
- Our CSI rating never changes.
- If you can do so much better, why don't you go try. Put your money where your mouth is.
- Profitability is all that matters.
- Customers are a dime a dozen. They can be easily replaced.
- We're running this business for us...not for them.

- We got an automated phone system to take care of all that.

- Customer service is as good as it always was.

- Quality is as good as it ever will be.

Blaming problems upon others:

- Our consultant told us to do it.

- We used to have a lot of business. Had a guy here who chased it off. (The "cash cow" switched companies.) Even though we don't have any business now, we still choose to blame him.

- Oh, that's a bunch of media hype.

- We're waiting to see what (governmental entity) will do.

- What's all this talk about organizational effectiveness? We're good at what we do. No need to change things because some outsider says so.

- People are expendable. If they don't like it, they can leave. Workers are easily replaced.

- Our accountant says we cannot do that right now.

- We've got to get to the base root of the problem...your attitude.
- With your behavior, you'll either be very successful or end up in jail.
- Our ad campaign backfired.
- The devil made me do it.
- We're too worried about _____ (some item in the news...the latest source of gossip).
- Interest rates are too high.
- Our lawyer can take care of any problems that arise. Until then, it's business as usual.
- Ethics and standards...those are for chumps. Making the big bucks is all that matters.
- Avoiding change, denying the need for change.
- What worked before works now...always will.
- Things will always stay the same here.
- Once the PR crisis passes, things will get back to normal.

- Can't change the weather or the world. So, why bother trying to change anything else.
- That's just the way he-she is. Learn to live with it.
- Our human resources department takes care of that.
- We're afraid of litigation.
- There's not a thing that we can do to change things. The status quo is perfectly acceptable.
- That's the way the cookie crumbles. That's life. What are you gonna do about it?

Not engaging in planning for future operations:

- So what are you gonna do about it?
- There's too much talk about planning. We're just busy doing things.
- We have a Mission Statement.
- All I have to do is dream. Dreams come true.
- Our track record should speak for itself.
- Money covers up a lot of ills.

- We have annual sales projections.
- My future is in your hands.
- Your future is in my hands.
- Good things happen to good people. It will be our turn soon.
- Surely, things will work themselves out.

When They Say........It Really Means........

It's our tradition.

The implication is that they've attained a plateau and no longer need to learn, grow or evolve. Just because something was done a couple of times, they are now calling it a "tradition." This is designed to stave off change or the need for re-evaluation.

Why can't you learn to compromise?

Do things their way.

What kind of training do you have to do this?

They're trying to either impress or intimidate you with credentials. Or, they may suggest that you're not properly trained to do what you already do successfully.

How did you get that project-assignment-client?

They figure that you must have known someone with an inside track. It couldn't have had much to do with your talent and expertise.

How do you get clients?

They want some fast-track answers so they can try them and receive direct benefit.

I want to be like _____ when I grow up.

Still have not found their own niche, self-esteem or purpose. Haven't learned yet that you cannot go through life as a carbon copy of someone else's public image.

Why don't you go write your life story?

They're uncomfortable with people who possess diverse accomplishments-talent-esteem. Some want to classify you as something you may have done well in the past but cannot acknowledge that you have moved forward. Some may poke holes at your body of work.

He's a good guy.

That person holds my beliefs, which are right and just. He-she is also someone from whom I want something or could benefit from association. People who are different are not to be acknowledged, accepted or tolerated. They're not good guys.

We don't have any problems here.

They're not willing to acknowledge problems truthfully. It's easier to scapegoat others who offer constructive criticism. A company or manager can only bury one's head in the sand for so long. After that, the truth of the messengers must be heard. Though constructive criticism and expert advising are tough to take at first, they are vital for continuous quality improvement.

You have my guarantee on it.

Customer service is presently at an all-time low. Companies will say anything to sell products, including building your "trust" in them. By having a commercial spokesperson issue a personal guarantee, you'll know they're one of the "good guys." This phrase is more a condemnation about the poor state of customer service than a slogan of a particular seller. It's an acknowledgement that the marketplace has profound problems with establishing-nurturing customer relationships and that trust is a novelty.

You have the education necessary to do the job. What more do you need?

Many managers throw employees into the water and expect them to swim, without giving lessons. They cannot and do not function in a mentor role because nobody did it for them (and likely didn't know how themselves). To turn bosses into coaches is a much-needed concept, but it cannot happen unless they want to become more than the supervisors they once had. Management by neglect is a continuum that proliferates the business culture. Managers do not know or won't admit to how much they don't know. Unless there's a desire to be something more, then the continuum will endure.

I took early retirement.

They may not have been viewed by the employer as longterm team players. May not really have contributed toward company goals and may have been released for good reason.

I didn't want to work for that company anymore. They weren't up to my standards.

It wasn't a good fit, for one party or the other. Too often, people want to place blame for something that was not destined to work out in the longrun.

The request for proposals was subsequently withdrawn.

All they really wanted to do was garner ideas, methodologies and information from proposing firms. Public sector agencies are notorious about putting proposers through the ringer. A large percentage of Requests for Proposals are bogus processes and contain unfair criteria.

Your proposal was rejected because the committee thought it did not meet the requirements.

Selecting the "successful proposer" was probably an "in job." The bureaucrats had someone else in mind but went through the Request for Proposals process as a formality or perhaps to steal ideas from over-eager proposers. If your proposal were different or offered new or creative ideas, it threatened the status quo of the "committee."

We now have some year-end budget money to spend, but the project has to be finished ASAP.

A mid-manager wants to look good on his-her year-end performance review or to justify a bonus. Thus, they want a quick-sizzle project to help them shine. This project will not go well for the executing contractor because it is not sufficiently prepared or ill-timed.

We're not ready to do this project at this time.

A mid-manager went hunting for a project but could not secure enough funding. Perhaps, that person was never fully authorized to begin the project in the first place but will not admit it publicly.

We have all the help we need. Our present consultants are taking care of everything.

The company cannot really distinguish one "consultant" from another. May have been scammed by one consultant who says that he/she can "do it all." Their corporate culture most likely does not really want to try new approaches and is afraid to seek out seasoned advice.

Can I have additional references?

If they didn't request references earlier, they are back-pedaling...trying to find a reason **not** to do the project. They are hoping the references will discredit or shoot the messenger of change. If they agree to work with you and request references after the fact, they may be afraid of what you represent (changes in the way they do business).

He's not my type. There's no chemistry.

I think I can do better. He does not have the outward qualities that I consider attractive. Never mind the inner qualities because I'm only interested in external appearances and cannot handle a deep communication relationship anyway.

So, what do you think about ____?

They are playfully challenging your status as an expert in your field. In humor lies a large degree of sarcasm. They may be jealous of your fame or expertise. So is the red flag word.

Common Sense Retorts to Sweeping Generalizations

Here are some of the common mis-statements

that people make. Some do so to avoid addressing the real business issues head-on. Others never had the rationales and their implications explained to them properly.

The savvy business executive or advisor will offer pro-active followups. Trite statements should not just sit as they are made. By responding realistically and with an eye toward company improvement, you'll be doing colleagues a service. Examples:

This company reflects the character of its CEO.

Sadly, that's true...to extremes. Many companies are ego-driven. The wise CEO is one who listens to others, surrounds himself-herself with smart people and fosters a spirit of teamwork. A good company is not predicated upon one personality but, instead, has adopted a corporate culture that thinks and feels.

Our company has got the most up to date computer hardware and software.

Companies spend disproportionate amounts of money on technology and neglect their people, processes and policies. Technology represents less than 1% of an organization's pie chart. Technology should be addressed as a tool of the trade...the bigger issues being a cohesive plan of action and organizational vision.

We must be doing something right.

Some companies succeed in their early stages because of raw energy. Conditions change...as should the companies. We must encourage colleagues to honestly examine reasons for their initial success and caution them that Continuous Quality Improvement is necessary. Companies must always grow to "the next tier" and not rest upon laurels.

If it ain't broke, don't fix it.

This is probably the worst cop-out. There is no organization that is totally perfect and cannot stand some fine-tuning. The process of Continuous Quality Improvement is for good companies which want to get better and move forward...a sign of wisdom. To adhere to the belief that nothing needs fixing is sheer stupidity.

We are a very quality-oriented company.

Quality is as quality does. Some organizations pay considerable lip service to quality but are clueless as to what it really is, what it means or how it can be sustained. There is no single standard of quality. It is customized and is a conscious, continuous effort to plan, think, act and measure. Quality is neither a quick fix for problems nor a shortcut to success and riches.

We know what our customers want.

This is usually said to challenge suggestions

that research, communications and better customer service might be necessary. Sadly, companies pay mostly lip service toward customer service. They don't stimulate enough dialog. When you suggest that a more targeted customer focus would benefit all, including their bottom line, management often gets pious, argumentative and confrontational. Or, they just look the other way, while the customers go elsewhere.

Success speaks for itself.

People who have temporarily high sales love to crow. To them, monetary volume is the "definition" of success. You should do business with them because they are a "winner," so they claim. In reality, no single market shift speaks completely for itself. Sales rankings vary, with various influencers. Many factors contribute toward longterm success, which is a road filled with ups and downs. Everything is subject to interpretation. Organizations must educate consumers, in a pro-active way, on how to best utilize their products-services.

Ways to Avoid Negative Euphemisms:

- Put more emphasis upon substance, rather than flash and sizzle.

- Look outside the organization, instead of keeping your total focus internal.

- Challenge negative comments and make

the accusers accountable for organizational progress.

- Keep communications open and continual.
- Refrain from making false representations.
- Abilities to think, reason, take risks and feel gut human instincts must all be nurtured.
- Take advise from all sources. Do your research. Get informed counsel from seasoned advisors.
- Document and comprehend reasons for successes. Cite case studies often.
- Empower the organization to embrace-embody the corporate culture.
- Learn to manage change, rather than become a victim of it.

6

Mis-Statements ... Slogans that Mis-Lead

Many Companies Over-Represent to Sell Something . . . and Believe Their Own Word Games

It is both comical and sad to analyze certain promotional hype that one hears. Some companies claim that purchasing their product is the "be all, end all" panacea for life's dilemmas. If only you will buy their version of "The Answer," then you can surely fast-forward your way to instant riches, success and an easy life.

This is not written to take swipes at responsible branding, marketing and advertising. More than 80% of what one sees and hears is clever, informative, research-based, sensibly executed and intended to orient target audiences toward marketplaces. Advertising fulfills many essential niche needs.

This is written to address the bigger issue that some companies believe the hype that they are issuing. One most often hears inflated mis-representations, false perceptions and over-statements via such contexts as:

- Corporate image spots that appear on TV news shows.
- Business-to-business publication advertising.
- Self-promotional brochures.
- Direct mailings to niche audiences.
- Catalogs.
- Cause-related marketing materials.

Some companies are downright parsimonious about themselves. Some either skillfully lie to get what they think they want...or may really believe themselves to be what they hype to publics who don't know any better.

Many consumers are gullible, "name" crazy and susceptible to grandiose claims. They take what is said at face value because they have not or don't care to develop abilities to discern what is hyped by others. They believe distortions faster than they believe facts, logic and reason.

This negatively impacts our society...which continually seeks button-pushing answers for life's complex problems without paying enough dues toward a truly successful life. Consumers naively believe mis-representations...to the exclusion of organizations which are more conservative, yet substantive, in their informational offerings.

Many of the hucksterisms represent "copywriting" by people who don't know anything about corporate vision. Their words overstate, get into the media and are accepted by audiences as fact. By default, companies have the appearance of credibility based upon mis-representations.

Companies put too much of their public persona in the hands of marketers and should examine more closely the distorted messages and partial images which they put into the cyberspace. Our culture hears and believes the hype, without looking beyond the obvious. People come to expect easy answers for questions they haven't yet taken the time to formulate.

Here are some examples of the misleading and mis-representing things one sees and hears in the Information Age:

Achieve perfection.

What they're really selling: Computer software.

My analysis: There is no such thing in life as perfection, as anyone who had led a meaningful life has learned. Continuous Quality Improvement is a higher level of thinking. Computer software is merely one tool out of many. It cannot single-handedly create quality.

Solutions for a small planet.

What they're really selling: Internet access.

My analysis: It takes more than a keyboard to effect solutions. You need global thinkers, planning, visioning, human interaction, the ability to reason...and much more.

Problem solvers.

What they're really selling: Computer technicians.

My analysis: Yes they are, for less than one tenth of one percent of business issues.

Helping you achieve your future.

What they're really selling: Photocopying equipment.

My analysis: You achieve your own future, with the help of skilled advisors. Once you strategize your life's plan, it is a good idea to share photocopies of it with others.

A better life for the people of ____.

What they're really selling: Electric power plants.

My analysis: Yes, but how community-responsive are the companies which sell equipment to public utilities. What is their commitment toward literacy, social services, health care, the environment, multicultural diversity and other key issues that really create a better life?

Work smarter, not harder.

What they're really selling: Computer software.

My analysis: Productivity software does no good unless one commits to change, alters behavioral traits and commits to time management. Then, we move on toward the bigger issues which software is not capable of addressing: what you do with your time, what you contribute and how you grow—succeed.

Tap the potential of companies focused on the future.

What they're really selling: Stock investments.

My analysis: The stock market looks primarily at profits...one small part (1%) of the business picture. It must also focus upon people, products, processes, procedures and potential.

How the Fortune 1000 made their fortune.

What they're really selling: Paging equipment.

My analysis: Pagers were not invented when they made their fortunes. Communications is fundamental to maintaining, but technology is only as good as the people using it. The bigger question is: how accessible are the executives, and how is company vision articulated and shared? That's the kind of communications that really grows companies.

Products for healthy living.

What they're really selling: Skin cream.

My analysis: An overstatement. Health care professionals rank other things higher on the list of priorities.

Your survival could depend on it.

What they're really selling: Home fire safety gear.

My analysis: Agreed, though I would include continuing education, self-fulfillment and the ability to plan one's future life to the equation.

Change your hairstyle as easily as you change your mind.

What they're really selling: Ladies' hairpieces.

My analysis: Many people (women and men) have trouble changing both...which still reflect the mindsets and self-images of their college days.

Speak the language of business success.

What they're really selling: Foreign language lessons.

My analysis: English is the international business language, and most people do not use it to best advantage. Workplace illiteracy is much more rampant than people even understand. Many managers have poor people skills, as well as poor verbal-written communications skills. Business writing and public speaking classes should be mandatory. The ability to communicate must be taught to all who wish to attain business success.

Develop the drive to accomplish anything.

What they're really selling: Motivational tapes.

My analysis: Agreed, in philosophy. They require human development, mentoring, knowledge enhancement and much more to be successful. Tapes alone are not enough. They may start or augment a path of self-growth and success. Tapes cannot take the place of reading.

Insightful advice for a complex world.

What they're really selling: Banking.

My analysis: Financial planning does not constitute global thought on life. It's 1% of the total picture. Banks buy money wholesale and sell it to borrowers at retail rates. Banks are now trying to compete with financial planners and investment banking houses.

Getting you back to the way things once were.

What they're really selling: Home owners' insurance.

My analysis: There is nothing more permanent and positive than change (which is 90% beneficial). Too many people spend much of their lives clinging to the past, fighting change and criticizing those who progress. While insurance is important, nothing should promise a return to the past. That plays into the hands of has-beens.

Enhancing your life at home.

What they're really selling: Outdoor signage.

My analysis: To facilitate enhancement, focus upon quality time with the family, hobbies, reading, exercise, gardening and entertaining guests.

The spirit of excellence.

What they're really selling: Residential real estate.

My analysis: Price and location are the deciding factors in real estate. Knowledge of the agents is the next factor. While all companies should achieve excellence in what they do, no single organization embodies it all.

Your opportunity of a lifetime is here. You owe it to yourself and your family to be successful.

What they're really selling: Multi-level marketing, home-based business.

My analysis: The language of infomercials often preys upon low-income and low-esteem people. It alleges that their scheme is the only true way to riches...which is a quick path toward a successful family life.

Obviously, they are mixing messages to sell their programs. Life is a series of progressions, choices, dues-paying and self-earned successes. There is no substitution for diligence and hard work.

Has all the trappings of a box office sensation.

What they're really selling: Trucks.

My analysis: That means that it's based upon flash, sizzle and hucksterism. This week's box office sensation will be forgotten soon enough. There's always another waiting to take its place.

Why do TV newscasts devote so much valuable airtime to show box office grosses for movies? That's not news.

Further, it reinforces the erroneous message that sales rankings are the primary measure of a company or product. Anybody who hangs their hat upon changeable, temporary rankings is headed for a fall.

The public also loves to see celebrities, products, trends and cultural icons fall just as quickly as they rise. It's a sick phenomena. Nothing—not even reputable films—should be judged only by fickle box office ratings.

Accelerate your business.

What they're really selling: Computer software.

My analysis: Not every company grows at the same rate. Database software does not make a company grow. It is a tool of people who put thought, planning, products and processes into perspective.

Computer "consultants" are not business strategists. Their product is one out of hundreds of business tools and must, therefore, be kept in proper perspective.

Improving health care in America.

What they're really selling: Data processing systems.

My analysis: Managing data and managing doctors (which is tough to do) are not the same thing. Non-core vendors do not and cannot improve the quality of a client's core business. Products and services assist the bureaucracy to do its job more efficiently but cannot claim credit for Big Picture success of a client's entire industry. In the case of health care, it's more of a societal phenomenon that goes beyond the controls of its industry, providers and vendors.

Brewing solutions for a better environment.

What they're really selling: Packaged beverages.

My analysis: It is misleading to list the charities one has supported in one's history, especially to prove a deceiving point. When you're in the business of manufacturing and marketing packaged beverages, it is misleading to suggest that you're in the business of protecting the environment. Cause related marketing is wonderful, but a company that exploits one cause may paint a partial (and thus false) picture of itself.

The Internet is fast becoming the greatest business revolution ever.

What they're really selling: Computer software.

My analysis: The Internet is a vehicle for sales

and marketing. History tells us that revolutions are never fast. For terms like "greatest," try practical experience, learning, planning and human communication with colleagues...qualities which a sales vehicle cannot provide.

The bumpy road to success made smooth.

What they're really selling: Small business banking services.

My analysis: Banking, like computer hardware and software, is a tool of the trade...not a driving force. Success is a long process, based upon how well one takes the turns. There are no shortcuts to true success.

Red Flag Expressions

"When you hear, beware of false claims!"

- Mission
- Family Tradition
- Fastest Growing
- Caring
- In One Easy Lesson
- Better
- #1 in Sales

- World Class
- Wealth and Riches
- The Best
- For All Your Needs

"Our mission."

What they're really selling: Retail merchandise.

My analysis: Beware of that phrase in advertising. It's a sales ploy. Retailers are motivated by keeping the cash registers ringing. It's unlikely that sales people know what a Mission Statement is and the Strategic Planning process are. To confuse sales and Big Picture messages is a travesty.

"Family tradition."

What they're really selling: Usually retailers, restaurants, service companies.

My analysis: If the founder is still active in the business and is accessible to customers, then the reputation is upheld. Dysfunctional family-run businesses reflect dysfunctional families. Hiring blood relatives, in-laws and old friends is not always good business. A few pull their share, and others coast on the certainty of nepotism. Research shows the odds are against family businesses going past a second generation, for these and other reasons. Tradition is a red flag expression because it implies that change has not occurred. Nobody does things exactly as they did in the early days. To say they do is deceptive to customers, employees and the good family name. Tradition and maintaining the status quo are two different concepts. Real tradition is predicated upon change management and steady evolution of the business.

7 Defeating signs for growth companies

When a company says they are the "Fastest Growing," beware! These circumstances are likely in place, each of which will defeat their claims:

1. Systems are not in place to handle rapid growth...perhaps never were.

2. Their only interest is in booking more new business, rather than taking care of what they've already got.

3. Management is relying upon financial people as the primary source of advice, while ignoring the rest of the picture (90%).

4. Team empowerment suffers. Morale is low or uneven. Commitment from workers drops because no corporate culture was created or sustained.

5. Customer service suffers during fast-growth periods. They have to back-pedal and recover customer confidence by doing surveys. Even with results of deteriorating customer service,

growth-track companies pay lip service to really fixing their own problems.

6. People do not have the same Vision as the company founder...who has likely not taken enough time to fully develop a Vision and obtain buy-in from others.

7. Company founder remains arrogant and complacent, losing touch with marketplace realities and changing conditions.

"Caring for the community."

What they're really selling: Perceived corporate self-image.

My analysis: Television stations are notorious about producing and airing self-serving promotional campaigns. They "care" about the community. The bulk of their "caring" is to promote local newscasts, which are their most lucrative sources of advertising revenue.

They say they are facilitating community dialog. Most available public service time, instead of going to non-profit organizations, is sold to corporations. Cause-related marketing packages have the "feel-good" look of public service but are really disguised ad campaigns to promote corporate agendas and produce more revenues for the TV stations.

Newspapers brag about all they donate toward educating the community. What they're really "donating" is unsold ad space. They make up profits by increasing rates of advertisers...offering cause-related marketing packages as incentives.

When one media insists upon having exclusive name rights to a special event, that's the kiss of death. For years, I've recommended to charities that they not put all their eggs in one basket. If one media is the "name sponsor," then that will negate coverage by other media. Charities rationalize that exclusivity gets them more intensive coverage than would a "shotgun publicity" approach...which is not true and has never been proven so.

Name media are also notorious about failing to give all the exposure that they promised...citing advertising commitments as the overriding factor. This is truthful because media companies are firstly in the business of running advertising. Running programming and local news coverage is just the "wrap-around" to generate audiences for advertisers. At the bottom of the totem pole sits coverage of community activities...unless they can sell advertising around it.

"In one easy lesson."

What they're really selling: A quick fix, or a quick way to get company buy-in.

My analysis: Meaningful strategy, improvement and change are not achieved via quick fixes. They also need not be long drawn-out processes. Reasonable timelines may be achieved. Company growth or success cannot be accomplished In One Easy Lesson because human beings require more than once to learn meaningful lessons...plus the time and attention necessary to put lessons learned to good use.

"Better."

What they're really selling: Their way of producing and selling.

My analysis: Human behavior training tells us that judgmental qualifiers like "good, bad, mean, evil and better" are self-defeating. To be better is to slam someone else.

"#1 in sales."

What they're really selling: You should buy from them, since so many others do.

My analysis: #1 is for now. Sales rankings constantly change. To buy only because a company hypes that they are #1 is not a valid reason. Buy what you want...from a company that you respect. Also, if they're #1, you're just another sales statistic and customer service will suffer commensurately to the numbers behind whom you must stand in line.

"World class."

What they're really selling: If you want to be associated with a winner, buy from them.

My analysis: The organization that claims "world class" is trying too hard to be put in the league of others.

"World class" is not self-bestowed...it is earned via a long track record.

"Wealth and riches."

What they're really selling: Their product is all that you need.

My analysis: There are no shortcuts to wealth and riches. Nobody will give away their secrets. Pyramid marketing schemes take advantage of failed hopes and ungrounded wishes. As P.T. Barnum once said, "There's a sucker born every minute."

"The best."

What they're really selling: Temporary rankings.

My analysis: There are too many ups and downs in business, without proclaiming yourself in a position for others to dispute or attack. Being successful in the longrun is much more admirable than being temporarily "the best."

"For all your needs."

What they're really selling: Wanna-be syndrome.

My analysis: No product or service fulfills all of a customer's needs. To suggest otherwise is narrow-minded. The more self-assured business makes long lists of what it doesn't do. It knows and relishes its niche, without trying to be all things to all people.

Now, to Salute Good Examples of Slogans, Company Posturing

As many misleading statements and campaigns

there are, I would like to cite some of the ones that I respect. These prove that marketing can be compelling, thought provoking and intriguing at the same time. Here are some that I salute:

Better grades are just the beginning. *Sylvan Learning Centers*. This illustrates that continuous quality improvement is a process, not a quick fix. I heartily agree that learning is the key to everything else in life and that it must be planned and nurtured.

The difference Is planning. *Merrill Lynch*. Agreed, although financial planning (a subset of Branch 3 on The Business Tree) constitutes less than 1% of full-scope organizational planning. If every consultant and vendor would advocate a cohesive approach to planning, directed toward a Big Picture, then organizations would run better and individuals would lead quality lives.

It's all in how you look at it. *The New York Times*. Bravo. Very insightful. Perspective is everything...continually changing, reflective and powerful for our future.

Look and you see the world around you. *Investor Owned Light and Power Companies*. If we age gracefully, we become more perceptive and enjoy life better. Otherwise, we stagnate. The choice is up to the individual (and any organization, as well).

Silence is acceptance. *Public service campaign to facilitate discussions about drug abuse*. Many families abdicate responsibilities for parenting to schools, the community or to anybody but themselves, Organizations reflect their own lack of training about people skills and management issues. They either cannot or won't try to teach what they were not taught. Managers tell employees what not to do and criticize them for being wrong. Yet, it's their fault because ground rules were not adequately communicated, nor has mentorship occurred. Doing nothing causes much more organizational damage than making mistakes while operating in good faith. Silence (followed by harsh criticism) is the worst way to communicate.

We make money the old fashioned way. We earn it. *Smith Barney.* Business is a process, not a sure thing. Companies which are prepared to "go the distance" will reap greater rewards, including financial.

Touches the lives of just about everybody. *General Electric*. If more companies thought of the implications of what they do upon multiple constituencies, they would do a better job. Don't think in the "micro." Think more "macro" about who decisions and policies affect.

Life is about learning. *Depends undergarments*. Absolutely. Maturity is a process. Too many young people don't know that, or care. Too many "mature" people have ceased to continue learning. The really wise ones learn each year...in a continuum of experiences.

The mantle of greatness cannot be earned in a single summer or in a decade. Greatness is

Earned over an entire career. *Rolex Watches*. Yes, indeed. Too many people want the acclaim of their seniors but are not willing to do the things that their seniors did to get there. Wanna-be's generally will not go the distance because they don't take the time to amass skills for success. Those who achieve longterm do so because of a plan to succeed, commitment to their profession, people skills, community stewardship, participation in mentorship, ongoing professional development, self-fulfillment and a positive attitude.

Characteristics of Good Slogans-Campaigns and, thus, Company Philosophy

- Focus upon the customer.
- Honor the employees.
- Show life as a process, not a quick fix.
- Portray their company as a contributor, not a savior.
- Clearly defines their niche.
- Say things that inspire you to think.
- Compatible with other communications.
- Remain consistent with their products, services and track record.

7

Hold On to What You've Got!

...The Biggest Customer Service Mistakes That Damage and Lose Business

Everyone with whom you do business is a customer or referral source of someone else. The service that we get from some people, we pass along to others. Customer service is a continuum of human behaviors...shared with those whom we meet.

Customers are the lifeblood of every business. Employees depend upon customers for their paychecks. Yet, you wouldn't know the correlation when poor customer service is rendered. Employees of companies behave as though customers are a bother, do not heed their concerns and do not take suggestions for improvement.

There is no business that cannot improve its customer service. Every organization has customers, clients, stakeholders, financiers, volunteers, supporters or other categories of "affected constituency."

Every employee is a customer of someone else's company. Theoretically, being the recipient of bad service inspires us to do better for our customers. The more that one sees poor customer service and customer neglect in other companies, the more we avoid the pitfalls and traps in our own companies. Unfortunately, it doesn't work out that way.

Customer service begins and ends at top management. If management is complacent or non-participatory, then the same philosophy is held by employees who render the service. If management insists upon Continuous Quality Improvement and demonstrates by its own actions, then service continually improves. All involved benefit from sensitivity toward customer needs, interests and concerns.

Or Else...Tally the Damages and Lose Customers

Having annual sales projections does not substitute for a cohesive and well-monitored customer service program. Training for employees is not a panacea for necessary long-term strategic planning...and by itself cannot replace customer service programming.

Just because you tried something pro-active once does not mean that it sticks, nor lasts forever. Continued fine-tuning, training and benchmarking are necessary.

These are the sure signs of self-defeating problems with companies that must be addressed with a customer service program:

- Having a bottom-line-only mentality.

- Squeezing every extra dollar, as if it's your God-given right to pursue greed.

- Failure to really listen to customers. Inability to read and hear between the lines.

- Condescension toward customers.

- Sloppy administrative handling of customer paperwork.

- Failure to initiate communications with the customer.

- Keeping the customer waiting unnecessarily.

- Giving the customer unsatisfactory explanations for things not done in a timely manner.

- When the customer has to prod your company to get action.

- Lying to the customer.

- Making the customer wrong.

- Never giving the customer anything value-added.

- Management pays lip service to quality...but does not "walk the talk."

- Company vision is not fully articulated, nor communicated and understood by all within the organization.

- Employees do not have a clue about the subtleties and sophistications of life...especially when their customer base is upscale.

- Taking inappropriate actions to repair the damage.

- Getting advice from the wrong consultants.

7 Reasons Why Nice People Do Not Get Good Customer Service

1. Basic Knowledge of What Good Service Really Is. They don't ask for it, are too naive toward flaws in the service provider's organization and don't know alternatives to request or demand.

2. Don't Realize Own Buying Power. Individuals are not fully aware of their customer status. They allow vendors to set the terms and knuckle under to companies' promises, half-truths and lies.

3. Limited Exposure to Excellence. The average person does not know what is considered Excellence in service, doesn't demand excellence and may not really want-desire excellence.

4. Buy the Company's Hype. The public believes that because certain companies are

high-profile, they are well-run and customer-sensitive companies. It is a trap to falsely equate marketing to goodwill or standards of quality.

5. Indifference. Many people and organizations are too shy to stand their ground for customer rights. They don't bother to state their case or set boundaries, thus, settling for mediocrity because they have not demanded quality.

6. Continue Being Nice about It. Consumers are generally not willing to write letters, speak to supervisors or make demands. They prefer to play the martyr but not assert their own position over vendors.

7. Continue to Accept Less Than the Best. Problems will indeed continue without correction. Most customers get upset but do not let people in authority know the basis for their frustration. And they continue going back to where shabby treatment was experienced, rationalizing the companies' mistakes away for them.

7 Ways to Lose Business...the Biggest Customer Service Mistakes Made

1. Forgetting Why You Are in Business. The company has failed to keep a clear focus upon the product, its marketplace, its customers and people who influence your company's ultimate success. Thinking is too limited,

applying "band aid surgery" and pursuing activity without a cohesive plan.

2. Failure to Retain Customers. Insensitive businesses figure that lost customers are easily replaceable. Research shows that retaining 2% more customers has the same effect upon the bottom line as cutting costs by 10%. A longtime customer is 2-3 times more profitable for the business than a recently added customer. Longtime customers make referrals, which reduce the company's marketing costs. Dissatisfied customers will tell 10-20 other people. Thus, the successful business must put the customer into a co-destiny relationship. Customers want to build relationships, and it is the obligation of the business to prove that it is worthy.

3. Deceiving the Customer. Failure to deliver what was promised is a cardinal sin. Other ways to deplete customer bases include bait and switch advertising, unexpected or unauthorized charges and occasions when the bill is substantially more than was quoted. Failure to handle mistakes and complaints in a timely, equitable and customer-friendly manner is inexcusable, and shifting the burden to automated "care centers" escalates the problem.

4. Order-Taking Mentality. Companies lose customers when the person taking the order delegates to others to fulfill in his-her absence, or when fill-in people rarely deliver as though

their livelihood depended upon it.

5. Lack of Service Orientation. Don't post a CSI rating unless you and every member of your team really know what it means. There must be a commitment to maintain it. Consumer complaints must launch a genuine action to improve. To avoid customer concerns and do business as usual is a mockery of the quality process. Such a company does not have the right to flaunt its perceived CSI rating any longer.

6. Poorly Trained Employees. Employees mirror management's philosophy. If they're only concerned with the cash register ringing, without giving any more, than they do not have a right to keep customers or stay in business. Workers in companies think and behave as though customers are necessary evils and tolerate them. This mindset kills any Vision or Big Picture thinking that company founders have built, as well as marketplace goodwill.

7. Lack of Participation by Management. If problems are handled through form letters, subordinates or ignored, then management is the real cause of the problem. Management must speak personally with customers to achieve understanding and set a good example for employees. Customers should "fire" management, rather than cashiers, secretaries and front-line personnel...going to the top to management with their problems and concerns.

Typical Excuses Given for Poor Service

Poorly run companies always want to make themselves right and the customer wrong. To them, customers are a pain in the neck and are supposed to understand their position and stop complaining. Customer service behaviors reflect a corporate culture that does not put clientele and marketplaces first.

These quotes are taken directly from customer surveys, "secret shopper" intelligence studies and my own observations and research. One could not make up a more ridiculous list of quotes. Sadly, all are true and reflect the poor level of customer service in business today.

Some of the worst rationalizations by service personnel:

Don't blame me. I'm just doing what I was told.

I'm not doing anything wrong. What's your problem?

It's our policy to _____.

Things are tough enough today. Like I really needed your problems.

Come back another day. Things will be better.

That's not my job. This isn't my work station. Wait until your assigned server gets here.

This isn't my regular job. I'm just filling in.

Those are the rules.

What do you say when people gripe to you all day?

Please understand...we've had a lot to do lately.

That's the way it is. If you don't like it, then take your business elsewhere.

Customers like you think you own the place. Where do you get off?

I don't work for you. I work for the company. My boss is satisfied by the job I do.

Looks like you woke up on the wrong side of the bed today.

There is nothing wrong with our company. So, what's your problem?

We're very busy at this time of year.

We sell the best products at the best prices. That should speak for itself.

Even worse -- and what sets the tone for bad service -- are retorts-excuses voiced by their supervisors:

We're very busy and understaffed right now. You must understand.

I'm sorry that you feel that way. But, that's the way it is.

I'm management, and our customer service people have the ability to behave as they wish.

Not everything is the way that I would like it to be.

What right do you have to complain? What are your credentials to judge the quality of service?

The boss doesn't give us enough resources. We're doing the best we can.

We always give quality service. I cannot understand why you feel otherwise.

He's so good in other areas. I cannot change his behavior just because you say so.

I have to work with him and cannot upset the boat. I will not say anything to him about this.

_____ refers him so much business. He cannot be all that bad.

That's management's policy, not mine.

Why don't you go back to the clerk and settle your grievance.

I understand that you have a problem.

We're Number One in sales. We must be doing something right.

Our customer service department handles all problems. See them.

We're operating according to company policies and procedures.

Our company is not broken. Why are you trying to fix it?

7 Cardinal Rules of Customer Service

1. It is Politically Incorrect to Make the Customer Wrong. Service personnel cannot appear "right" at the customer's expense. They are there to serve and, more importantly, to collaborate in the customer's satisfaction.

2. Everyone Makes Mistakes. The mark of Quality is how you handle them. Learn the art of diagnosing problems, taking customer input and effecting workable solutions.

3. Sales and Service Are Not the Same Package. People with sales expertise must develop customer service orientation. Know the difference and train on both.

4. Businesses Live or Die By the Customers. If you think otherwise, then you do not have the right to remain in business.

5. Attitude Affects Everything in Business. Customers and other stakeholders know when it is sincere. They support a company that tries

harder and resent one that does not.

6. Good Service is Nurtured, Not Edicted. It doesn't just happen. Good customer service is the end product of experience and training. Employees must want to participate and continually improve. Consistency, resources and support assure the company's success.

7. Corporate Arrogance is Unacceptable. Management has the obligation and responsibility to see and deal with things as they are...not as they would like them to be. Otherwise, they are fooling themselves and letting customers and the entire organization down.

Hold On to What You've Got...what you think you've got...what you actually have.

Research and understand what the marketplace thinks you've got...in relation to customer needs. Keep what you've earned...what you think you've earned and what you've actually earned. Keep gains by demonstrated behaviors that reinforce customer service. Study and fully comprehend how other companies lose business. Profit from their mistakes.

No company can grow without giving quality service. Unmanaged growth is not good growth. Understand the high costs of recovering from losses and catching up lost marketplace.

Offer "Value-Added" to customers. Excellence and partnering with customers ("Potlache") is yet another step beyond adding value. Thank customers for past business and reap loyalty and referrals. Business must continually re-earn customers' future business.

The roles and responsibilities of every organization executive and each member-employee must relate to customer service. This cannot be abdicated to other people, least of all a machine. The pomposities of a business which is out of touch will catch up.

8

Been There, Done That ...

People Often Say They Have...But Really Haven't

How to Pick the Right Consultants for Your Company

Selecting the most appropriate consultant for your company -- optimizing expertise -- is the greatest challenge facing a decision maker.

It's lonely at the top. Certain kinds of objective information cannot come from within your own camp. True expertise is a rare commodity, and the successful company utilizes it on the front end, rather than on the costly back end.

Matching consultants with actual and emerging company needs is the corporate leader's quest. With a wealth of expertise available via outsourcing, one can quickly become a "kid in a candy shop," wanting whatever is readily available or craftily packaged.

Too many consultants mis-state and over-represent what they do, stemming from:

- Eagerness to get business.
- Short tenure in consulting, believing that recent corporate experience readily translates to the entrepreneurial marketplace.
- Unfamiliarity with the actual practice of consulting at the executive level.
- Lack of understanding about business needs, categories, subtleties and hierarchies.
- Failure to create service area niches and target clients.
- Professional rivalry with other consultants, resulting in the "I can do that" syndrome.

Everyone knows that dentists, nurses, social workers and respiratory therapists are all health care professionals. Yet, distinctions in their expertise lead consumers to discern and seek out specialists...or at least ask a general practitioner physician to make referrals for necessary services.

Niche consultants place emphasis in the areas where they have training, expertise and staff support for implementation...and will market their services accordingly. An accounting firm may suggest that an economic forecast is a full-scope business plan (which it is not). A trainer may recommend courses for human behavior, believing that these constitute a

Visioning process (of which they are a small part). Marketers might contend that the latest advertising campaign is equivalent to re-engineering the client company (though the two concepts are light years apart).

Niche consultants believe these things to be true, within their frames of reference. They sell what they need to sell, rather than what the client really needs. Let the buyer beware.

Consultants Are Not All Alike

Distinctions must be drawn into three consulting categories (and percentages of their occurrence in the marketplace):

1. Vendors sell products which were produced by others. Those who sell their own multiply produced works are designated as subcontractors. (82.99%)

2. Consultants conduct programs designed by their companies, in repetitive motion. Their work is off-the-shelf, conforms to an established mode of operation, contains original thought and draws precedents from experience. (17%)

3. High level strategists create all knowledge in their consulting. It is original, customized to the client and contains creativity and insight not available elsewhere. (.01%)

As one distinguishes past vendors and subcontractors, there are six types within the 18% which constitute consultants (with their percentages in the marketplace):

1. Those who still lead in an industry and have specific niche expertise. (13.5%)

2. Those who were downsized, out-placed or decided not to stay in the corporate fold and evolved into consulting. (28%)

3. Out of work people who hang out consulting shingles in between jobs. (32%)

4. Freelancers and moonlighters, whose consultancy may or may not relate to their day jobs. (16%)

5. Veteran consultants who were trained for and have a track record in actual consulting. That's what they have done for most of their careers. (2%)

6. Sadly, there is another category...opportunists who masquerade as consultants, entrepreneurs who disguise their selling as consulting, people who routinely change niches as the dollars go. (8.5%)

99.999% of actual management consultants come from five basic career orientations and fit onto one of the five branches of **The Business Tree:**

1. Technical or niche industry orientation

2. Financial
3. Entrepreneurial, small business management
4. Academic, research
5. Human resources management

The remaining 1/1000 of a percent of consultants is a rare breed...a Big Picture strategist, fitting onto Categories 6 and 7 (trunk and roots of **The Business Tree**). The Corporate Strategist is an idea person who has run businesses, knows about all other categories, deals in concepts and policies, and possesses sophisticated understanding and insight.

What They Claim They Do

When They Say They Provide, They're Usually

Growth strategies—Sales trainers
Company turnaround—Marketers
Information for business solutions—Accountants

Choosing Consultants

These pointers are suggested in the selection of business advisors and consultants. Ask a true business strategist to help you to determine which consultants are needed, draft the requests for proposals, evaluate credentials and recommend contracting options.

Understand what your company really needs and why. Don't pit one consultant against another, just to get free ideas.

Don't base the business on "apples to oranges" comparisons.

Ask for case studies which were directly supervised by the person who will handle your business...not stock narratives from affiliate offices or a supervisor. Find out their expertise in creating and customizing for clients...rather than off-the-shelf programs which they simply implement. Determine their abilities to collaborate and interrelate with other consultants.

In budgeting for and pricing consulting services, budget for consulting at the start of the fiscal year, averaging 10% of gross sales. This does not include marketing, which should be another 10%.

See consulting as an investment (short-term and long-term), not to be short-changed. Every size of business needs consultants, just as your clients need your services. The company which makes the small investment on the front end (consulting) saves higher costs. Research shows that consulting fees foregone are multiplied six-fold in opportunity costs each year that action is put off.

Consulting fees are best compensated by the hour. The client who contracts a quantity of time may request a volume discounted fee. It is customary to pay for all consultations after the initial "get acquainted" session.

Out-of-pocket expenses are customarily passed through to clients, without markup. For project purchases, such as printing, graphic production, video production and materials creation, consultants customarily mark up slightly, to cover bank financing and handling costs.

Questions to Consider in Evaluating Consultants Include:

- Would you feel comfortable if they ran your company?
- What is their longevity? Were they consultants 10-20 years ago? Real consultants must have at least a 10-year track record to be at all viable as a judgment resource.
- What is their maturity level? Could they appear before a board of directors?
- How do they meet deadlines, initiate projects and offer ideas beyond the obvious?
- If one level of consultant sells the business, will this same professional service your account? Big firms usually bring in junior associates after the sale is made. Demand that consultants of seniority staff the project.
- How consistent are they with specific industries, types of projects and clients?
- How good a generalist are they? Consultants with too narrow a niche will not ultimately serve your best interests.

Professional status is important. Prospective clients should inquire about the consultant's respect among current and recent clients and reputation among affected constituencies within the business community. Look at their activity in professional development and business education. If they do not pursue a program of ongoing knowledge progression, they are obsolete and not valuable to clients.

Also examine potential consultants regarding their own track record at mentoring other business professionals. Check to see that they give beyond the scope of billable hours. Pro-bono community involvement is a factor because it indicates character, ethics and integrity. If they have done little or none, they are not worth hiring. Top professionals know the value of giving back to the community that supports them, becoming better consultants as a result.

The Ideal Consultant:

- Clearly differentiates what he/she does...and will not presume to "do it all."

- Is a tenured full-time consultant, not a recently down-sized corporate employee or somebody seeking your work to "tide themselves over."

- Has actually run a business.

- Has consulted companies of comparable size and complexity as yours.

- Has current references and case histories.

- Gives "value-added" insight...in contrast to simply performing tasks.

- Sees the scope of work as a professional achievement...rather than just billable hours.
- Pursues client relationship building...as opposed to just rendering a contract service.

9

Collaborations, Partnering and Joint-Venturing

...the Fastest-Emerging Priority for Business

The biggest source of growth and increased opportunities in today's business climate lie in the way that individuals and companies work together.

It is becoming increasingly rare to find an individual or organization that has not yet been required to team with others. Lone rangers and sole-source providers simply cannot succeed in competitive environments and global economies. Those who benefit from collaborations, rather than become the victim of them, will log the biggest successes in business years ahead.

Just as empowerment, team building and other processes apply to formal organizational structures, then teamings of independents can likewise benefit from the concepts. There are rules of protocol that support and protect partnerships...having a direct relationship to those who profit most from teamings.

Definitions of these three terms will help to differentiate their intended objectives:

Collaborations—Parties willingly cooperating together. Working jointly with others, especially in an intellectual pursuit. Cooperation with an instrumentality with which one is not immediately connected.

Partnering—A formal relationship between two or more associates. Involves close cooperation among parties, with each having specified and joint rights and responsibilities.

Joint-Venturing—Partners come together for specific purposes or projects that may be beyond the scope of individual members. Each retains individual identity. The joint-venture itself has its own identity...reflecting favorably upon work to be done and upon the partners.

Here are some examples of **Collaborations**:

- Parties and consultants involved in taking a company public work together as a team.
- Niche specialists collectively conduct a research study or performance review.
- Company turnaround situation requires a multi-disciplinary approach.
- A group of consultants offer their collective talents to clients on a contract basis.

- The client is opening new locations in new communities and asks its consultants to formulate a plan of action and oversee operating aspects.
- Professional societies and associations.
- Teams of health care professionals, as found in clinics and hospitals.
- Composers and lyricists to write songs.
- Artists of different media creating festivals, shows and museums.
- Advocate groups for causes.
- Communities rallying around certain causes (crime, education, drug abuse, literacy, youth activities, etc.).
- Libraries and other repositories of information and knowledge.

Here are some examples of **Partnering**:

- Non-competing disciplines create a new mousetrap, based upon their unique talents, and collectively pursue new marketplace opportunities.
- Widget manufacturing companies team with retail management experts to open a string of widget stores.

- A formal rollup or corporation to provide full-scope professional service to customers.
- Non-profit organizations banning resources for programs or fund-raising.
- Institutions providing startup or expansion capital.
- Managing mergers, acquisitions and divestitures.
- Procurement and purchasing capacities.
- Corporations working with public sector and non-profit organizations to achieve mutual goals in the communities.
- Private sector companies doing privatized work for public sector entities.
- Organ donor banks and associations, in consortium with hospitals.
- Vendors, trainers, computer consultants and other consultants who strategically team with clients to do business. Those who don't help to develop the business on the front end are just vendors and subcontractors.

Here are some examples of **Joint-Venturing**:

- Producers of energy create an independent drilling or marketing entity.

- An industry alliance creates a lobbying arm or public awareness campaign.

- Multiple companies find that doing business in a new country is easier when a consortium operates.

- Hardware, software and component producers revolutionizing the next generation of technology.

- Scientists, per research program.

- Educators, in the creation and revision of curriculum materials.

- Distribution centers and networks for retail products.

- Aerospace contractors and subcontractors with NASA.

- Telecommunications industry service providers.

- Construction industry general contractors, subcontractors and service providers in major building projects.

- Group marketing programs, such as auto dealer clusters, municipalities for economic development, travel and tourism destinations, trade association and product image upgrades.

- International trade development, including

research, marketing, relocation, negotiations and lobbying.

Situations Which Call for Teams to Collaborate

1. **Business Characteristics:** Most industries and core business segments cannot be effectively served by one specialty. It is imperative that multiple disciplines within the core business muster their resources.

2. **Circumstances:** People get thrown together by necessity and sometimes by accident. They are not visualized as a team and often start at cross-purposes. Few participants are taught how to best utilize each other's respective expertise. Through osmosis, a working relationship evolves.

3. **Economics:** In today's downsized business environment, outsourcing, privatization and consortiums are fulfilling the work. Larger percentages of contracts are awarded each year to those who exemplify and justify their team approaches. Those who solve business problems and predict future challenges will be retained. Numerically, collaboration contracts are more likely to be renewed.

4. **Demands of the Marketplace:** Savvy business owners know that no one supplier can "do it all." Accomplished managers want teams that give value-added, create new ideas and work effectively. Consortiums must con-

tinually improve, in order to justify investments.

5. **Desire to Create New Products and Services:** There are only four ways to grow one's business: (1) sell more products-services, (2) cross-sell existing customers, (3) create new products-services and (4) joint-venture to create new opportunities. #3 and 4 cannot be accomplished without teaming with others.

6. **Opportunities to Be Created:** Once one makes the commitment to collaborate, circumstances will define the exact teaming structures. The best opportunities are created.

7. **Strong Commitment Toward Partnering:** Those of us who have collaborated with other professionals and organizations know the value. Once one sees the profitability and creative injections, then one aggressively advocates the teaming processes. It is difficult to work in a vacuum thereafter. Creative partnerships don't just happen...they are creatively pursued.

What Collaborations Are NOT:

- Shrouds to get business, where subcontractors may later be found to do the work.

- Where one partner presents the work of others as their own.

- Where one party misrepresents his-her capabilities...in such a way as to overshadow the promised team approach.
- Where one partner treats others more like subcontractors or vendors.
- Where one participant keeps other collaborators away from the client's view.
- Ego fiefdoms, where one participant assumes a demeanor that harms the project.
- Where cost considerations preclude all partners from being utilized.
- Where one partner steals business from another.
- Where non-partners are given advantageous position over ground-floor members who paid the dues.
- Where one or more parties are knowingly used for their knowledge and then dismissed.

Who Wants to Collaborate:

- Those who have not stopped learning and continue to acquire knowledge.
- Those who are good and wanting to get progressively better.

- Those who have captained other teams and, thus, know the value of being a good member of someone else's team.

- Those who do their best work in collaboration with others.

- Those who appreciate creativity and new challenges.

- Those who have been mentored and who mentor others.

- Those who don't want to rest upon their laurels.

- Those who appreciate fresh ideas, especially from unexpected sources.

Who Does NOT Want to Collaborate:

- Those who have never had to collaborate, partner or joint-venture before.

- Those who don't believe in the concept...and usually give nebulous reasons why.

- Those who think they're sufficiently trained and learned to conduct business.

- Those who want only to be the center of attention.

- Those who fear being compared to others of stature in their own right.

- Those who think that the marketplace may not buy the team approach.

- Those who are afraid that their process or expertise will not stand the test when compared with others.

- Those who had one or two bad experiences with partnering in the past...usually because they were on the periphery or really weren't equal partners in the first place.

Characteristics of a Good Collaborator:

- Already has a sense of self-worth.

- Has a bona fide track record on their own.

- Have a commitment toward knowledge enhancement.

- Walk the Talk by their interactions with others.

- Supports collaborators in developing their own businesses, offering referrals.

- Have been on other teams in the past...with case studies of actual collaborations.

- Have successes and failures to their credit...with an understanding of the causal factors, outcomes and lessons learned.

Stages of Relationship Building for Business Partners

1. **Want to Get Business:** Seeking rub-off effect, success by association. Sounds good to the marketplace. Nothing ventured, nothing gained. Why not try!

2. **Want to Garner Ideas:** Learn more about the customer. Each team member must commit to professional development...taking the program to a higher level. Making sales calls (mandated or voluntarily) does not constitute relationship building.

3. **First Attempts:** Conduct programs that get results, praise, requests for more. To succeed, it needs to be more than an advertising and direct marketing campaign.

4. **Mistakes, Successes & Lessons:** Competition, marketplace changes or urgent need led the initiative to begin. Customer retention and enhancement program requires a cohesive team approach and multiple talents.

5. **Continued Collaborations:** Collaborators truly understand teamwork and had prior successful experiences at customer service. The sophisticated ones are skilled at building and utilizing colleagues and outside experts.

6. **Want and Advocate Teamwork:** Team members want to learn from each other. All

share risks equally. Early successes inspire deeper activity. Business relationship building is considered an ongoing process, not a "once in awhile" action or marketing gimmick.

7. **Commitment to the Concept and Each Other:** Each team member realizes something of value. Customers recommend and freely refer business to the institution. What benefits one partner benefits all.

Evaluating Collective Working Relationships

I have observed the greatest successes with collaborations, partnering and joint-ventures to occur when:

- Crisis or urgent need forced the client to hire a consortium.
- Time deadlines and nature of the project required a cohesive team approach.
- The work required multiple professional skills.
- Consortium members were tops in their fields.
- Consortium members truly understood teamwork and had prior successful experiences in joint-venturing.
- Consortium members wanted to learn from each other.

- Early successes spurred future collaborations.
- Joint-venturing was considered an ongoing process, not a "once in awhile" action.
- Each team member realized something of value.
- The client recommended the consortium to others.

My own disappointments with previous collaborations include:

- Failure of participants to understand—and thus utilize—each other's talents.
- One or more participants have had one or a few bad experiences and tend to over-generalize about the worth of consortiums.
- One partner puts another down on the basis of academic credentials or some professional designation that sets themselves apart from other team members.
- Participants exhibit the "Lone Ranger" syndrome...preferring the comfort of trusting the one person they have counted upon.
- Participants exhibit the "I can do that" syndrome...thinking that they do the same exact things that other consortium members do and, thus, see no value in working together, shar-

ing projects and referring business.

- Junior associates of consortium members want to hoard the billing dollars in-house...to look good to their superiors, enhance their billable quotas or fulfill other objectives that they are not sophisticated enough to identify.

- Junior associates of consortium members refuse to recognize seniority and wisdom of senior associates...utilizing the power of the budget to control creative thoughts and strategic thinking of subcontractors.

Here are the reasons to give the concepts of Collaborating, Partnering and Joint-Venturing a chance:

- Think of the "ones that got away"...the business opportunities that a team could have created.

- Think of contracts that were awarded to others who exhibited a team approach.

- Learn from industries where consortiums are the rule, rather than the exception (space, energy, construction, high-tech, etc.).

- The marketplace is continually changing.

- Subcontractor, supplier, support talent and vendor information can be shared.

- Consortiums are inevitable. If we don't do it early, others will beat us to it.

Benefits for participating principals and firms include:

- Ongoing association and professional exchange with the best in respective fields.
- Utilize professional synergy to create opportunities that individuals could not.
- Serve as a beacon for professionalism.
- Provide access to experts otherwise not known to potential clients.
- Refer and cross-sell each others' services.
- Through demands uncovered, develop programs and materials to meet markets.

These are the truisms of collaborations, partnering and joint-ventures:

- Whatever measure you give will be the measure that you get back.
- There are no free lunches in life.
- The joy is in the journey, not in the final destination.
- The best destinations are not pre-determined in

the beginning, but they evolve out of circumstances.

- Circumstances can be strategized, for maximum effectiveness.

- You gotta give to get.

- Getting and having are not the same thing.

- One cannot live entirely through work.

- One doesn't just work to live.

- As an integrated process of life skills, career has its place.

- A body of work doesn't just happen. It's the culmination of a thoughtful, dedicated process...carefully strategized from some point forward.

- The objective is to begin that strategizing point sooner rather than later.

10

You've Got to Be Taught

Making Training Work for Your Organization

Training is the most important ingredient in corporate development. Today's workforce will need three times the amount of training that it now gets...if the organization intends to stay in business, remain competitive and tackle the future successfully.

Each year, one-third of the Gross National Product goes toward cleaning up problems, damages and the high costs of doing either nothing or the wrong things. Half of that amount goes toward some form of persuasion, instruction, spin-doctoring or educating.

More often that not "training" is a vehicle to tout one's viewpoint, tinker with old problems or blame someone else for the course of events. If training is viewed as band-aid surgery to fix problems, then it will fail. Managers who have this "fix those people" mindset are, in fact, the ones who need substantive training the most.

Training is rarely allowed to be extensive. It is usually technical or sales-marketing in nature. Employees and executives are rarely mentored on the people skills necessary to have a winning team. Thus, they fail to establish a company vision and miss their business mark.

Outside of "think tanks" for company executive committees, full-scope education does not occur. This is primarily because niche trainers recommend what they have to sell, rather than what the company needs. Niche trainers impart their own perspectives out of context to the whole of the organization.

Team building must be part of the corporate Vision first, not as a series of exercises delegated to trainers. I conduct Executive Think Tanks for corporate management. The success of this enables trainers with the "rank and file employees" to be optimally successful. Organizations of all sizes must have the Think Tank...which delineates future operations, including education and training.

Training is unfairly blamed and scapegoated for pieces of the organizational mosaic that Strategic Planning and cohesive corporate Vision should have addressed early-on. Trainers cannot reconstruct organizational structure, nor can other niche consultants.

Companies owe it to themselves to think and plan...before launching piecemeal training programs. After carefully articulating and understanding direction, then training needs (including team building and empowerment) will stand a chance of being successful.

7 Steps Toward Professional Development

1. Teaching-Training. Conveying information, insights and intelligence from various sources. Categorized by subject, grade level and methods of delivery. Expert teachers (fountains of learning material) are the building block in the educational process, and the student must be an active participant (rather than a non-involved or combative roadblock).

2. Studying. One cannot learn just by listening to a teacher. Review of material, taking notes, seeking supplementary materials and questing to learn additionally must occur.

3. Learning. The teacher instructs, informs and attempts to enlighten. The student accepts, interprets and catalogs the material taught. Periodically, the material is reviewed.

4. Information. As one amasses years of learning, one builds a repository of information, augmented by experiences of putting this learning into practice.

5. Analysis. One sorts through all that has been learned, matched with applicabilities to daily life. One determines what additional learning is necessary and desired. From this point forward, education is an ongoing process beyond that of formal schooling. If committed, the person turns the quest for knowledge into a life priority.

6. Knowledge. A Body of Knowledge is derived from years of living, learning, working, caring, sharing, failing and succeeding. This step is detailed in my monograph, "The Learning Tree": (1) Life. (2) Living Well. (3) Working Well. (4) Education. (5) Philosophy. (6) Self Fulfillment. (7) Purpose and Commitment.

7. Wisdom. This requires many years of commitment to learning, compounded by the continuous development of knowledge. Few people attempt to get this far in the educational process. Those who do so have encompassed profound wisdom. This step is detailed in my monograph, "7 Layers of Wisdom": (1) Glimmer of An Idea. (2) Learning Curve. (3) Applications for Lessons Learned. (4) Trial and Error, Success and Failure. (5) Teaching, Mentoring. (6) Insights, Beliefs, Systems of Thought. (7) Profound Wisdom, Life Perspectives.

7 Levels of Training

1. Basic Education. There are certain things that every member of the workforce needs in order to do jobs well. These include people skills, operational duties and requirements for each job description.

2. Mandated. Circumstances (usually regulators) insist that such training be conducted as the basis for getting or retaining funding. Progressively, mandated training tends to be

utilized in these stages: (1) Fix Those People. (2) Stay Where You Are...and Don't Lose Further Ground. (3) This Is the Way It Is...Things We Have to Live With. (4) Accept Somebody's Pet Project. (5) Things "They" Are Making Us Do. (6) What We Want to Teach You. (7) You'll Do It, and You'll Like It.

3. Informational. This category enlightens workers on new ways to accomplish old tasks. It introduces new policies, procedures, concepts and directions in which the organization will pursue. In this category, workers are encouraged to offer suggestions for improvement and become part of the quality process.

4. Technical, Niche Skills. There are hundreds of categories of "technology," and each requires training and experience in order to maximize the job tasks. Providers of such training come from a plethora of niche specialties, both inside and outside the company.

5. Procedural. Every organization must create, fine-tune and benchmark the processes by which it produces products-services. Process administration and procedural adherence assure consistencies.

6. Optional. Not every facet of running a successful company can be reduced to a process or technology. People need attention, enrichment, accountability, rewards and room to grow. It is at this level that Professional Development (a

higher order than training) must take over. Every worker's quest to spread his/her wings must be developed. Most executives were never taught how to be real executives, and this arena for Executive Mentoring must become a company priority. Alas, these areas are not really "optional."

7. Insightful-Deep-Rich-Meaningful. Learning and growing professionally pre-empts burnout. Develop a Strategic Plan for your company and yourself. Participate in CEO think tanks. Mentor others, and reconnect with those whom you admire. Invest in the right consultants. Commit to a quality improvement program. View your company as part of a career Body of Work, not just a present job. Levels of Training That Are Rare But Truly Needed: (a) Pride in Workmanship. (b) Learning, Growing, Mentoring. (c) Fully Actualized Professionalism. (d) Amassing People Skills. (e) Pursuing Excellence. (f) Adding Value to the Organization. (g) Developing a Body of Work-Knowledge.

Categories of Training Which Company Programs Should Encompass

There is a difference between how one is basically educated and the ingredients needed to succeed in the longterm. Many people never amass those ingredients because they stop learning or don't see the need to go any further. Many people think they are "going further" but otherwise spin their wheels.

There is a large disconnect between indoctrinating people to tools of the trade and the myriad of elements they will need to assimilate for their own futures. Neither teachers nor students have all the necessary ingredients. It is up to both to obtain skills, inspiration, mentoring, processes, accountability, creativity and other components from niche experts.

Therein lies the problem. Training vendors sell what they have to provide...not what the constituencies or workforces need. Emphasis must be placed upon properly diagnosing the organization as a whole and then prescribing treatments for the whole, as well as the parts.

Training should be conducted within a formal, planned program that addresses the majority of organizational aspects, per categories on **The Business Tree**™ :

1. **The business you're in**
   Core industry
   Subject experts
   Emerging trends
   Product design

2. **Running the business**
   Making products-services in an efficient manner
   Technical instruction
   Technological innovation
   Telephone etiquette
   Time management
   Physical plant operations instruction
   Computer operations, training, programming, repairs

Telecommunications operations and maintenance
In-service exercises, per organizational task
Re-engineering of processes
Administrative practices, procedures, operations, structure, review
Equipment, supplies, systems
Relationships with suppliers, vendors
Distribution

3. **Financial**
Accounting practices
Banking practices
Payables and receivables administration
Insurance and benefits program administration
Purchasing
Forecasting, budgeting
Investor relations
Taking companies public
Mergers, acquisitions, expansion opportunities

4. **People**
Learning organization
Empowerment
Team building
Human relations skills
Recruiting, hiring and supervision of employees
Stress management
Negotiating skills
Leadership development
Professional development
Executive development
Re-engineering of policies and procedures
Re-engineering of the workforce

5. **Business Development**
   Business and marketplace development
   Developing sales programs and strategies
   Sales training
   Marketing
   Advertising
   Public relations
   Research
   Corporate communications
   Working with graphic artists-providers, audio-visual companies, printers
   Special events planning-implementation
   Specialty advertising
   Direct marketing-research-telemarketing
   Collaborating to build new business opportunities

6. **Body of Knowledge**
   Company performance reviews
   Big Picture views of company structure...the interrelationship of Branches 1-5
   Professional development as a whole for the organization
   External influences and information
   Company general meetings, functions and overall events plan
   Government, regulators, marketplace limitors
   Community standards, opposition, support, constituencies
   Entering new industries, product lines, creating additional products-services
   Collaborations, joint venturing

7. **The Big Picture**
   Building a shared vision
   Strategic planning
   Outside-the-box thinking
   Executive Think Tanks
   Crisis management, preparedness
   The quality process
   Ethics
   Creative business practices, collaborations, innovations
   Changing markets, opportunities, barriers
   Walking the talk

7 Biggest Misconceptions About Training

1. One Size Fits All. If it's not customized, it's not going to be effective.

2. Trainers Are Business Experts. Generally, they are vendors who sell "off the shelf" products that target small niches within the organization. Few are schooled in full-scope business culture and have not been previously engaged to advise organizations at the top.

3. Human Resources Oversees Training. By their nature, HR departments are designed to uphold processes and systems. Training is about change, which contradicts the basic construction of HR. Not all HR people are versed in the subtle nuances of people skills and are, thus, not the best to supervise training. It really should not be under the thumb of HR.

4. Trainers Write the Training Plans. All major departmental plans should be written objectively and in concert with the Strategic Plan...by qualified advisors. Training companies often give free assessments in order to sell their programs. Free surveys do not constitute a cohesive plan. Let trainers do what they do best: training. Let experienced planners design the training plan, with input from trainers included. Don't let the plan evolve from a training company's sales pitch.

5. Only Industry Experts Can Train in Our Company. What companies need most is objective business savvy and sophisticated overviews. Core industry "experts" only know core industry issues from their own experiences. Quality training must focus on dynamics outside the core business yet should have relativity to the organization.

6. One Course Will Fix the Problem. Training is not a punishment for having done something "wrong." It's a privilege...a major benefit of employment. It unlocks doors to greater success, growth and profitability...for those trained and for the sponsoring organization. In order to be competitive in the future, today's workers will need three times the training that they are now getting.

7. That It's Supposed to Be Popular. The biggest mistake that meeting planners make is determining the effectiveness of training and train-

ing professionals via audience survey. Most conference evaluation forms are lightweight and ask for surface rankings...rather than for nuggets of knowledge learned. Speakers and training budgets are therefore judged upon whimsical comments of individual audience participants...which get harsher when the training is for topics they need, rather than things they would "prefer" to hear. Voices of reality are always criticized by people who really are not qualified to assess them.

Evaluating Training Providers

These pointers are suggested in the selection of training providers: Ask a senior business advisor to help determine which consultants are needed, write the training program, evaluate credentials and recommend contracting options. Understand what your company really needs and why. Don't pit one consultant against another, just to get free ideas. Don't base the training decisions on "apples to oranges" comparisons.

These pointers are suggested in budgeting for and pricing services: Budget for training at the start of the fiscal year, averaging 10% of gross sales. See training as an investment (short-term and long-term), not to be short-changed. Every size of business needs training. The company which makes the small investment on the front end (training) saves higher costs later.

The ideal training provider:

- Clearly differentiates what he/she does...and

will not presume to "do it all."

- Is a tenured full-time consultant, not a recently down-sized corporate employee or somebody seeking your work to "tide themselves over."
- Has actually run a business.
- Has consulted companies of comparable size and complexity as yours.
- Has current references and case histories.
- Gives "value-added" insight...in contrast to simply performing tasks.
- Sees the scope of work as a professional achievement...rather than just billable hours.
- Pursues client relationship building...as opposed to just rendering a contract service.

Your Company Needs More Than Just Training

I would like to see these additional topics added to the Professional Development and Company Visioning programs, extending the concept of executive training:

- Marketplace factors outside your company—how they can hurt or help your business.
- Generational work ethics and why young peo-

ple need executive mentoring to "go the distance" in their careers, offering value to the company and profession.

- Understanding the value of conducting independent company assessments, other than the "bean counter" approach.

- Workplace literacy. Much of the work force does not have basic skills, nor reasoning abilities. They embrace technology, rather than ideas and concepts.

- Understand and celebrate diversity. This is a blessing, not a mandate.

- Accept and embrace change. Research shows change is 90% beneficial. So why do people fight what is best for them?

- What business the company is really in...why...where they are headed...with what resources-knowledge-skills...on what timeline...who plays a part in growth...and how (the process known as Visioning).

- Learning how to control change, rather than fear it.

- Steps to create company vision...and get buy-in from employees.

- What makes good companies go bad.

- How to take planning and quality management from the esoteric and into daily practice.

7 Biggest Benefits of Training

1. Measurements. Test scores, grades, class rankings, GPA, SAT, professional certifications, licensing examinations, juried awards. Whether in school or business, we are all measured. Knowledge helps to make and predict society's measurements which are expected.

2. Thinking-Reasoning Skills. What we learn is important. Further, what we do with lessons, how facts are interpreted, how we approach problems and the faculties of common sense are vital to economic, social and self-betterment success.

3. Socialization-People Skills. Through trial-and-error, success-and-failure and the observation of other people's strengths-and-weaknesses, we learn how to live and work with others. Mastering people skills makes for win-win propositions.

4. Professional Development. Education does not stop after the highest degree completed...it merely begins. Training, professional enrichment, membership in associations and constructive business interaction are vital for career longevity and economic independence.

5. Mentorship. Learning from others takes a higher plateau when under the wings of experts. Mentorship (which has seven levels) is a stairstep process of bettering all participants. Meaningful lessons, paying dues and developing relationships empower those who make the effort "go the distance." Learning from different, unusual and informed sources is the art of mentorship.

6. Earning Power. Education (formal schooling, professional development and enhanced-relationship study) has a direct relationship to financial rewards. It begins with school but bears fruit in the willingness to learn, change and grow professionally.

7. Future Life. A truly successful person commits to mentoring others, giving back, mastering change and never failing to learn. Education is more than confirming one's held beliefs. It plants knowledge roots, which sprout in ideas, applicabilities and lifelong insights.

I recommend that team building training be conducted as part of a company Strategic Plan, with top management participating. Companies must plan...predicting (rather than reacting to) strengths, weaknesses, opportunities and threats.

Professional development must be offered to every employee, including mentoring for top executives and up-and-coming young people. Education should show decision makers all phases of the organization and what it takes to succeed and grow, personally and as a team.

11

Lessons Learned But Not Soon Forgotten

100 Ways for Executives to Succeed Longterm

Everything we are in business stems from what we've been taught or not taught to date. A career is all about devoting resources to amplifying talents and abilities, with relevancy toward a viable end result.

Amassing a **Body of Knowledge**—which leads to **Wisdom**—is a long and enjoyable process. It is the first step toward a career-life **Strategy**, which evolves into a **Vision**. Using a corporate analogy, a Mission Statement is 1% of a Strategic Plan, which is 20% of a Visioning Program.

Business evolution is an amalgamation of thoughts, technologies, approaches and commitment of the people, asking such tough questions as:

1. What would you like for you and your organization to become?

2. How important is it to build an organization well, rather than constantly spend time in managing conflict?

3. Who are the customers?

4. Do successful corporations operate without a strategy-vision?

5. Do you and your organization presently have a strategy-vision?

6. Are businesses really looking for creative ideas? Why?

7. If no change occurs, is the research and self-reflection worth anything?

Most of us learned about business (which is a compendium of life relationships) "in the streets." Today's business leaders entered and pursued careers without a a strategic plan or service manual.

Professionals pursue many approaches to garnering information and, ultimately, to unlocking the answers that inevitably lie within. Methods include seminars, books, consultations, professional association involvement, training, organizational development, executive roundtables, civic activities, etc.

Failure to prepare for the future spells certain death for businesses and industries in which they function. The same analogies apply to personal lives, careers and Body of Work. Greater business awareness and heightened self awareness are compatible and part of a wholistic journey of growth.

None of us can escape those pervasive influences that have affected our lives. Like sponges, we absorbed information and perceptions of life that have helped mold our business and personal relationships.

What I Learned

The most significant lessons that I learned in my life from mentors, verified with experience, include:

1. You cannot go through life as a carbon copy of someone else.

2. You must establish your own identity...which is a long, exacting process.

3. As you establish a unique identity, others will criticize. Being different, you become a moving target.

4. People criticize you because of what you represent, not who you are. It is rarely personal against you. Your success may bring out insecurities within others. You might be what they cannot or are not willing to become.

5. If you cannot take the dirtiest job in any company and do it yourself, then you will never become "management."

6. Approach your career as a Body of Life's Work. This requires planning, purpose and commitment. It's a career, not a series of jobs.

7. The person who is only identified with one career accomplishment or by the identity of one company for whom he-she formerly worked is a one-hit wonder and, thus, has no Body of Work.

8. The management that takes steps to "fix themselves" rather than always projecting problems upon other people will have a successful organization.

9. It's not **when** you learn. It's **that** you learn.

10. Most people do without thinking because they don't really develop thinking skills.

11. Analytical and reasoning skills are extensions of thinking skills.

12. You perform your best work for free.

13. People worry so much what others think about them. If they knew how little others thought, they wouldn't worry so much.

14. Fame is fleeting and artificial. The public is fickle and quick to jump on the newest flavor, without showing loyalty to the old ones, especially those who are truly original. Working in radio, I was taught, "They only care about you when you're behind the microphone."

15. The pioneer and "one of a kind" professional has a tough lot in life. It is tough to be first or

so far ahead of the curve that others cannot see it. Few will understand you. Others will attain success with portions of what you did. None will do it as well.

16. Consumers are under-educated and don't know the true substance of a pioneer. Our society takes more to the copycats and latest fads. Only the pioneer knows and appreciates what he-she really accomplished. That reassurance will have to be enough.

17. Life and career include peaks and valleys. It's how one copes with the "down times" that is the true measure of success.

18. Longterm success must be earned. It is not automatic and is worthless if ill-gotten. The more dues one pays, the more you must continue paying.

19. The next best achievement is the one you're working on now...inspired by the Body of Knowledge to date.

20. The person who never has aggressively pursued a dream or mounted a series of achievements cannot understand the quest-mission of one with a deeply committed dream.

21. A great percentage of the population does not achieve...but admires and learns from those who do persevere and succeed. The achiever thus becomes a lifelong mentor to others.

22. Achievement is a continuum, but it must be benchmarked and enjoyed along the way.

Lessons Which Can Only Come from Wisdom

These are some of the lessons that I learned after age 40 but wish I had learned earlier:

23. The more that you know, the more you need to know. The more you learn, the more you want to learn.

24. It is a true professional who can tell people what he-she does not know and points in the direction of niche experts. Wanna-be's say they always know more than the next person and can do it all.

25. People who often say, "Been there, done that" usually have not.

26. There will be no peace, empowerment or true professional cooperation unless there is a willingness to try and make collaborations work.

27. All of us agree on 95% of the issues. It's that 5% where we disagree that gets reasonable people into conflict.

28. When you squeeze the lemon into a glass of tea or water, cup it with one hand, and squeeze at an angle toward you. When you squeeze straight down, juice flies outward and usually

hits someone else.

29. The best quick cure for clothing stains from food is to squeeze a few drops of lemon.

30. The worst violators of "restaurant etiquette" are the people who work there. It's sad when you have to dodge them and be subjected to poor people skills, then be expected to give a large tip.

31. In "telephone etiquette," the person who opens the conversation by asking how you are is trying to sell you something.

32. In "telephone etiquette," the worst violator is the person who answers after hours...usually the boss.

33. Most people are not paid what they're really worth. If they were paid what the marketplace says they're worth and had to live by benchmarks, they would do a much better job. Thus, one must act as though his/her name is on the door.

34. People who hold jobs and people who pursue careers are different breeds. The twain rarely meet.

35. People don't really "win" lotteries. The money goes toward their administration and feathering their political nest. The same is true for many other quick-fix or hype public sector projects.

36. Full equality, justice and fairness does not exist in society. It can only exist in your heart.

37. When you leave something for repair, write and leave a full description of the problems. Do not give long, rambling explanations to repair people because they will reduce your comments to two words which do not adequately diagnose the situation.

38. Most people who call themselves "consultants" are ill-prepared, have never really "been there" and charge you to get them some experience or dollars. Look beyond the obvious in evaluating consultants.

39. Don't expect clerical people to run your issue, comment or concern up the flagpole. It is not their job because they are busy administering the office. Either speak to the supervisor or put it in writing to his-her supervisor.

40. Government and public sector bureaucracies do not want new ideas or more effective ways to operate. It's nothing personal against you or your expertise. Bureaucracies are predicated upon protecting their turf and their jobs.

41. Change is 90% positive. So why do people fight what is most beneficial to them?

42. The worst line spoken is: "It ain't broke, don't fix it." The next worse is: "We must be doing something right." People use these to ration-

alize the status quo and avoid confronting their own shortcomings. There is no organization that cannot be improved...just a little bit.

43. There is no such thing as perfection. The better philosophy is Continuous Quality Improvement. Set and exceed standards. Move the yardstick farther each time.

44. The only kind of conflict resolution that lasts is a **win-win**.

Lessons Learned...But Not Soon Forgotten

Fine-tuning one's career is an admirable and necessary process. It is not torture but, indeed, is quite illuminating. Imagine going back to reflect upon all you were taught. Along the way, you reapply old knowledge, find some new nuggets and create your own philosophies.

To help in retreading old lessons and augmenting with new ones, these are some pieces of advice to mid-level and upper executives:

45. Executive development is a finely tuned art. It is a tireless yet energizing process.

46. People who rise in upper corporate ranks do so for reasons other than themselves. The art is to understand and work with those factors, rather than to become a pawn of them.

47. The old ways of rising to the top have changed. The savvy executive masters the new ways.

48. Don't become a "flavor of the month." Trends and fads in business and in people will subside. Posture yourself for the longrun.

49. Develop and trust your gut instinct. It's right most of the time.

50. Senior level consulting is not something that one retires or down-sizes into. It is not a part-time profession or something that one does in between jobs. Few corporate executives have what it takes to be a consultant.

51. One is not a full-fledged consultant until he/she has done this and only this for 10 years. One does not become "senior" without at least a 20-year consulting track record, not counting working at jobs for someone else.

52. Preventive actions pay back original investments, 6-10 times. Remediate downward spirals, sooner rather than later, to remediate **The High Cost of Doing Nothing**™ .

53. Organizations get blamed for all consequences, including abuse, neglect, suffering and mistakes.

54. Management always wants to assign blame to someone else and success to themselves. They say, "Fix those people." The organization will not grow and mature until management realizes they are "those people."

55. People don't know why they believe in something. They just believe.

56. Never forget where you came from.

57. A fast-lane relief for stress is to slow down.

58. A house divided against itself will fall.

59. Society builds up idols only to shoot them down.

60. People believe lies more readily than they comprehend and absorb truths.

61. We mostly control our own destiny. Each time we abdicate, blame, relinquish or do nothing, opportunities pass by...**The High Cost of Doing Nothing**™ . Missed opportunities compound and can never be fully regained.

Teachings Available to All of Us

There have been many truisms of life within our own consciousness. Most were taught to us at early ages. Going back to reflect puts them into today's perspective and utilization:

62. Do unto others, as they do unto you.

63. It's as important how you end a relationship as how you begin it.

64. There is nothing more permanent than change.

65. Not everything changes at once. There's an orderly transition.

66. What's old becomes new again.

67. As things change, they meld with those which do not change. This new equation still constitutes change.

68. You get out of something what you put into it.

69. In order to get, you have to give.

70. You cannot always pick your family members.

71. Caring and sharing is a lifetime art.

72. Nothing worth having comes easy.

73. Plan to make mistakes...and how you will handle them.

74. Everyone makes mistakes. It's more important to know how you correct problems.

75. Sticking one's head in the sand is not an option.

Slogans in Daily Life

Along the way, we heard many song lyrics, slogans and concepts which, if reflected in a contemporary context, have deeper implications for business and life:

76. Drive to stay alive.

77. Drive friendly.

78. Let the sunshine in.

79. Please be kind. Rewind.

80. Life is a song worth living. Why don't you sing it!

81. The pause that refreshes.

82. My mama told me...you better shop around.

83. The show must go on.

84. There's a sucker born every minute.

85. The beat goes on.

86. Try to remember.

Behaviors, Per Ideologies

There is a distinction between the things which people instinctively know to do and the things they choose to do in daily transactions:

87. People know to shake packets of sugar-sweetener before adding to coffee-tea but forget to offer a drink to others before consuming.

88. Insincere respectful language and behavior toward one's elders is inconsistent, forced and comes across as contrived. Good manners should be an ongoing art of social behavior and courtesy to others...second nature, not an act.

89. The people who complain about customer service in retail establishments often give the worst considerations themselves to others in the workplace.

90. Customers who have been legitimately wronged usually do not or cannot speak up for themselves. When some do, it baffles businesses and makes them uneasy. Customers must find the confidence to challenge vendors for poor service.

91. People believe in speaking the truth. As it fits the purposes, the truth sometimes gets skewed.

92. People believe lies more quickly than they recognize the truth.

93. Truth is not always easy to recognize and not always pretty.

94. The bigger the lie, the more likely are more people to believe it.

95. Fight for and with the truth.

96. Citizens do not give as much back to their communities as they claim they do.

97. People who do not place a high value on their own time will not value others' time.

98. People judge others just as harshly as they appraise themselves.

99. Professionals who bill highly by the hour are the worst at getting other professionals to do "extra work" for free...not according the same professional courtesy.

100. Those who complain the most about not getting their "just deserved" (money, respect, power) have not paid enough dues to "get theirs" and likely never will.

12

Oxymorons

Studies in Conflicting Terminology

We hear them everywhere, especially in business. Things are said and believed to be true. Organizations which perpetuate myths and inconsistencies set themselves up for failure.

This appendix chapter, both for fun and sophisticated insight, puts forth several contradictory terms and business ideologies.

The dictionary's definition of **oxymoron**: "A combination of contradictory or incongruous words. Pointedly foolish."

Judge for yourself the realities of each term and cliche phrase in business usage:

Courtesy booth
Picture of perfect health
One size fits all

Common sense
Free money
Cruel kindness
Responsible behavior
Neighbors who know you
Gentle giant
Low-cost provider
Economy car
Planned serendipity
Child-like qualities
The Great American Novel
Rest room
Family values
Public servant
Computer logic
Low bidder
Military orderliness
Get rich quick
White House crisis
Special commission
Executive privilege
Profit motive
Youthful maturity
Pointedly dull
Careful listening
Good scissors
Genuine imitation
Best on Earth
Sales quotas
Good for you
Public spirited
Law and justice
Low-salt
Service station

Bank draft
Low cholesterol
Efficiency in government
Equal opportunities
Fair and just
Liked by everyone
Hated by everyone
Gift of gab
Plan as you go
Perfect marriage
Popular boss
Quick fixes
Ease and convenience
Justice for all
Matter of life and death
An hour-long TV show
Free earth
Doctors' bedside manner
Bring out the big guns
Dead to right
Good__music
Constructive criticism
Just like the rest

Oxymorons in the Business World

Sales and service as equal corporate priorities
Organization that doesn't need to grow any further
Saying everything that needs to be said
People knowing what is expected of them in their jobs
Business that puts environmental concerns first
Simple solutions for business problems
Customer friendly service
Micro-niche professionals who become company leaders

Personal attention from an automated telecommunications system
"This page intentionally left blank"
People whom you think can and will do things as well as you do
Outside-the-box management thinking
Companies with flexible rules-policies
Low-cost insurance that covers everything
Nothing to hide
Fixing problems for free
Temporary tax increase
Objective planning by internal people
Interim financing
Lotteries benefiting the taxpayers
Re-engineering
Seeing the customer's point of view
Work party
Born with leadership potential
One-man crew
All-inclusive concept or policy
Partially completed
People-friendly products
Clearly misunderstood
Doing things for all the right reasons
Random logic (fuzzy logic)
Responsible discord
Free publicity
Knowing all they need to know
The perfect plan
Having it all together
Original thinking
Unlimited resources
Crisis management
Big-Picture management

Mandatory option
Designed with you in mind
Global village
Quality at the lowest cost
Free legal advice
Mid-managers taking risks
Original copy
Fully developed listening skills
Exact estimate
Equipped to handle any situation
Committee decision
Having all the answers
Artificial intelligence
Payment for performance
Say what you mean
All the opportunities in the world
Mean what you say
Veteran consultant
Walk the talk
Taught them all they know
Amateur expert
Living in the Real World
Good, fast and cheap
Affordable health insurance
Budget shortfall
Fast results with little effort
Unacceptable solution
User-friendly computer
Fast-track bureaucrat
Full control
Idiots' work
Knowing exactly how someone feels
Creative accounting
Have them eating out of your hand

The best is none too good
Government planning
Job security
Working vacation
Standard deviation
Flexible freeze (economics)
Advanced basic
Faster, cheaper and better
Computer learning

Other Oxymorons

Act naturally
Government organization
Sanitary landfill
Airline food
Great Depression
Scheduled spontaneity
Almost exactly
Green forest
Second best
Alone together
Guest host
Secret FBI Files
Athletic scholarship
Half-full, half-empty
Silent music
Baby grand (piano)
Heart healthy gourmet food
Silent scream
Bad sex
Holy war
Singular relationship
Black light

Honest crook
Small crowd
Brief survey
Hopelessly optimistic
Software documents
Broadcast journalism
Hospital food
Sounds of silence
Butt head
Ideal situation
Student teacher
Buyer's market
In-depth TV reports
Sure bet
Child-proof
Industrial park
Sweet sorrow
Children's encyclopedia
Irate patient
Synthetic natural gas
Civil War
Jumbo shrimp
Taped live
Classic novel
Junk food
Terribly nice
Clean waterways
Lean pork
Terribly pleased
Code optimization
Legally drunk
Tight slacks
Computer jock
Light-Heavyweight

Turbo diesel
Computer security
Live on tape, live recording
12-ounce pound cake
Concise dictionary
Living dead
White chocolate
Congressional ethics
Marijuana initiative
Criminal justice
Medium-Large
Criminal lawyer
Metal woods
Deafening silence
Mild Abrasive
Death benefits
Military Intelligence
Deficit spending
Minor disaster
Definite maybe
Mobile home
Diet ice cream
Mobile station
Divorce court
Natural childbirth
Down elevator, down escalator
New classic
Dry wine
New wave of nostalgia
Efficiency in government
No-good do-gooder
Elementary calculus
Non-stop flight
Evaporated milk

"Now, then ..."
Even odds
Old news
Extra time
Organized mess
Family vacation
Passive aggression
Fast idle
Peace force
Fat-free
Peacekeeper missile
Fat-free ice cream, margarine
Perfect idiot
Found missing
Plastic glasses
Freezer burn
Political correctness
Fresh frozen
Political science
Friendly argument
Political will
Friendly fire
Pretty ugly
Golf fashions
Resident alien
Good grief
Safe sex
Gourmet pizza
Same difference

13

The Book of Acronyms

New Ways of Looking at Familiar Words

Re-defining Key Business Terms By What They Potentially Represent.

Organizations are accustomed to looking at concepts and practices one way at a time. Clinging to obsolete definitions and viewpoints have a way of perpetuating companies into downward spirals.

By viewing from others' viewpoints on life, we find real nuggets of gold with which to redefine organizations. Companies that adopt new viewpoints and defy their conventional definitions will create new opportunities, organizational effectiveness, marketplaces and relationships.

As a Big Picture strategist, I encourage new ways of thinking about old processes, including those which brought past and enduring successes. Symbolic are these phrase definitions which I have created for familiar business words. I have created new acronyms for well-known business terms, in order to help us visualize opportunities differently.

My acronym for BUSINESS:
Big-picture
Understanding of
Symbiosis
In
Nomenclature,
Economics,
Systems, and
Services

WORK:
Windows of
Opportunity,
Requiring
Know how

My acronyms for GOALS:
Getting
Organized
Allowing
Lifeblood
Systems

Growth
Opportunities
And
Legacy
Support

THINK:
To
Have
Ideas,
New
Keys

FAILURE:
Finding
Answers
In
Life,
Utilizing
Retrospective
Enlightenment

SETBACK:
See
Experiences in
Terms of
Business
Accomplishments,
Commending
Knowledge

SUCCESS:
Sophisticated
Utilizing of
Conditions,
Contributions,
Energies,
Strengths and
Synergies

My acronyms for FEAR:
Find
Excellence
After
Reflection

Formulating
Energies
Actions and
Responsibilities

TECHNOLOGY:
Teaching
Excellence
Can
Have
Numerous
Outcomes on the
Life
Of the
Global
You

WEB:
Worthwhile
Economical
Business

E-MAIL:
Enlightening
Marketplaces
And
Initiating
Links

PAST:
Perspectives
And
Systematic
Thoughts

FUTURISM:
Fully
Utilized
Thinking...
Underscoring
Retrospective
Insights...
Synergizing
Metholodogies

AWARD:
Amazing
Wins
Are
Really
Deserved

PLANNING:
Process to
Learn
Alternatives,
Narratives,
Notations, and
Insights
Necessary for
Growth

TEAM:
Training and
Education...
Always
Meaningful

QUALITY:
Quintessential
Understanding of
Actions,
Linkages, and
Information
Taught to
You

My acronyms for VISION:

Valuable
Intelligence
Search
In
Organizational
Networks

Viewing
Ideas,
Systems,
Insights and
Occasional
Newness

STAR:
Super
Talent,
Acting
Responsibly

DECISION:
Duty for
Executives to
Communicate
Issues,
Symbolisms, and
Important
Organizational
Necessities

SPEECH:
Sophisticated
Presentation
Equates
Enlightenment,
Communication and
Harmony

ETHICS:
Enlightened
Thinking...
Holding
Ideologies,
Commitments,
Sensitivities

My acronym for E-MAIL:
Enlightening
Marketplaces
And
Initiating
Learning

The purpose of any business is not just to make money. It is to be JUST:

- Committed to customers.
- Respectful of employees.
- Successful enough to grow, pay its dues and continue growing.
- Upholding standards of quality and commitment.
- Focused through everything else we back to our customers.

Too often, one hears about what goes wrong in business relationships. From our viewpoint, if business is conducted honorably and professionally, then profitability and success flow from doing the right things...not from pursuing false goals.

The best successes are earned and learned. We should not take good fortune for granted. Business track records are garnered by going the distance, reading the trends and continually changing.

As the years go by, one continues paying dues. Learning, experiencing and evaluating is the best process to achieve lasting success. The best dues yield nuggets of wisdom that couldn't have been earned any other way.

The smartest person is the one who knows what he-she does not know. With maturity comes the quest to learn more, understand the factors and apply newly acquired insights to higher purposes. The person who commits to a path of professional development never stops achieving...and profitably impacts his-her business relationships.

Language is food for the mind. Browse a dictionary, and you create new ideas. Words are fun and connect your business to tomorrow. Technology cannot take the place of human communication...only may add to it. Every opportunity should be taken to enhance literacy skills of employees and entire organization. The language of success is initially found in a dictionary.

My acronyms for EDUCATION:

(Standpoint of Students:)	*(Standpoint of Teachers:)*
Earning	Each
Distinction	Day
Usually	Unleash
Capitalizes	Creativity
After	After
Training and	Teaching and
Instruction	Inspiration
Optimize	Occur
Net-rewards	Noticeably

MUSIC:
Masterfully
Utilizing
Symbiosis,
Imagination and
Congruence

HEALTH:
Honoring
Excellence
Allows
Leadership
Toward
Humanity

IDEAS:
Individualized
Dimensions,
Expectations,
Analyzes,
Scenarios

FINANCE:
Formulating
Information,
Notations
And
Newly
Changing
Efficiencies

RESEARCH:
Reasoned
Enlightenment,
Seeking
Education
And
Responsibly
Connecting
Hypotheses

TRUTH:
Teach
Realities
Uniformly
Through
Harmony

COMMUNITY:
Citizens
Offering
Missions,
Methodologies,
Unification,
Needs and
Interconnections
To
You

MEETING:
Minds
Exercising
Effectiveness
Through
Ideas,
Negotiating
Goals

MONEY:
Mounting
Organizational
Necessities
Equal
Yields

BROKER:
Business
Resource for
Opportunities and
Keywords for
Economic
Rewards

SELL:
Skillfully
Explaining,
Linking
Language

Seeking
Enlightenment...
Listening and
Learning

CHANGE:
Continually
Having
A
Natural
Guidepost
Effect

DIVERSITY:
Different
Ideas,
Visions,
Energies,
Realities,
Symbolisms and
Insights
Throughout
You

ADVISOR:
A
Dedicated
Visionary
Inspires
Sophisticated
Organizational
Realities

LEARNING:
Legacy
Encompasses
All
Resource
Narratives...
Introducing
Noticeable
Galvanization

KNOWLEDGE:
Kaleidoscopic
Nucleus
Of
Weighed
Learning...
Embracing
Development,
Growth and
Effervescence

WISDOM:
We
Influence
Society
Due to
Our
Mastery

RESPECT:
Responsibilities
Epitomize
Sophisticated
Perspectives,
Earning
Commensurate
Truths

TRAINING:
Teaching
Radiant
And
Innovative
Nourishment
Inspires
Natural
Growth

LISTEN:
Language
In
Studying
The
Evident
Networks

PROBLEM:
Polarizing
Routine
Obstacles
By
Letting
Elegance
Materialize

SERVICE:
Securing
Excellence
Requires
Visualizing
Innovative
Customer
Effectiveness

PROGRESS:
Pursuing
Royal
Objective
Gages...
Rewarding
Empowered
Super
Service

FORTUNE:
Future
Operations
Require
Teams
Understanding
Needs and
Expectations

INNOVATE:
Imagining
Niches and
Norms,
Optimizing
Valuable
Alliances,
Training and
Experiences

REWARDS:
Reap
Expectations
With
A
Resilient,
Durable
System

Every business, company or organization goes through cycles in its evolution. At any point, each program or business unit is in a different phase from others. The astute organization assesses the status of each branch on its Business Tree™ and orients its management and team members to meet constant changes and fluctuations.

Going "outside the box" to shift perceptions enables any company to think, plan and operate in productive new ways.

Characteristics of Creative Business Definitions...thus, Company Philosophy.....

- Focus upon the customer.
- Honor the employees.
- Show business life as a continuous quality process (not a quick fix or rapid gain).

- Portray their company as a contributor (not a savior).
- Clearly define their niche (not trying to be all things).
- Say things that inspire you to think.
- Compatible with other company activities and behaviors.
- Remain consistent with their products, services and track record.

14

The Fine Art of Failure

A Leadership Primer on Benefitting from Mistakes We Make, In Order to Assure Success

Success and failure...it's a matter of perspectives. Out of every 10 transactions in our lives, five will be unqualified successes. One will be a failure. Two will depend upon the circumstances. If approached responsibly, they will become successful. If approached irresponsibly, they will turn into failures. Two will either be successful or will fail, based strictly upon the person's attitude.

A 90% success rate for a person with a good attitude and responsible behavior is an unbeatable percentage. There is no such thing as perfection. Continuous quality improvement means that we benchmark accomplishments and set the next reach a little further.

Throughout our lives, we search for activities, people and meaning. We venture down roads where we find success. Other activities bring us failure...from which we learn even more what to do to achieve success the next time.

We learn three times more from failure than from success. The longer that success takes to attain has a direct relationship to how long we will hold onto it.

Success is easily attainable. So, why do people psyche themselves into failing more often they have to...especially when they succeed much more often than they give themselves credit for.

Let a mistake occur, and the stream of remarks starts flowing: "We failed. They'll blame it on me. It's not my fault. There must be a traitor someplace. Once again, I screwed up. I can't seem to do anything right. Just my luck to get saddled with a bunch of idiots who don't know what they're doing. Does anyone know how to do this the right way? Hasn't anybody ever taught them?"

Sadly, there are elements of truth in explosive remarks. The bigger question is how people's mindsets toward mistakes and failures got that way.

7 Degrees of Failure...Plateaus in the Learning Curve

1. Education-Growth—Didn't know any better. Made some dumb mistakes, based upon incorrect assumptions, insufficient information or lack of sophistication to "see beyond the obvious." Beginning to learn better approaches by analyzing the wrong ways of doing things.

2. Evolution—Tried some things that worked

and some that didn't work. Beginning to understand that things do not fail without a reason or cause. Learns constructively from trial and error. Visualizing patterns of failure...as barriers to success.

3. Experience Gathering—Circumstances within and outside your control caused the projects to fail. Learns which external factors to trust and which cannot be controlled. The importance of research, due-diligence and marketplace understanding surface.

4. Grooming—The team let you down...understand why. Learns what you are capable of doing. Learns who to work with and in which capacities. Success-failure is a function of seizing-creating your own opportunities. No individual or organization can have success without experiencing and learning from failures.

5. Seasoning—Understand outcomes before they transpire...and the myriad of failure-producing factors. Most people and organizations fail due to never having control over certain ingredients, improper planning and the inability to change.

6. Meaningful Contributions—Attitude is everything...affecting the approach to problems. People say they fear failure the most, when they, in fact, sabotage their own opportunities for success. Develops sophisticated understanding of attitudes, behaviors and interper-

sonal skills as the motivator to convert failures into bigger successes.

7. Body of Knowledge—With time, seasoning, leadership development and a career track record, one experiences repeated successes and failures. Develops better understanding of cause-effect ratios. Develops profound insights and lifelong perspectives into the teachings of success and failure (learning three times more from failures than success).

Understanding and Comprehending Failures

Failing to meet objectives and believing that you have failed in life and work are two different perspectives. I reviewed a 20-year segment of my career, working with professionals who helped me to formally analyze. From a "time and motion" perspective, we found that considerable time was wasted on the wrong projects, non-supportive work environments, the wrong mix of clients and conditions for providing advise-counsel.

Through the review, I learned that my "failures" at time-intensive projects shined light on what I was better suited to do: generate wisdom and foster the enthusiasm for top executives to see things differently. A seeming failure to manage time and motion was ultimately a success in the many revelations that occurred.

My frustrations with menial "busy work" projects (just to produce billings and pay the salaries of other people) crystallized into insightful recollections, such as the one you are now reading. From a value perspective, among the wasted hours (due-diligence administrative work) were gems of wisdom that I later abstracted and polished into a series of books. The light bulb would not have shined if I hadn't learned the lessons through experience.

We learn from the failures of all people and organizations around us. Looking in the third person enables self-reflection. How would we handle things if they happened to us? Playing "what if" helps us think through situations and be better prepared to handle when they arise.

Why We Must Fail...in Order to Succeed

Learning the stumbling blocks of failure prepares one to attain true success. Fear is the biggest contributor to failure, and it can be a motivator for success. You cannot make problems go away, simply by ignoring that they exist.

Everybody fails at things for which they are not suited. The process of learning what one is best suited to do is not a failure...it is a great success. Learn from the best and the worst. People who make the biggest bungling mistakes are showing you pitfalls to avoid.

Many of us make the same mistakes over and over again. That is to be expected and teaches us volumes, preparing us for success. There is no plan that is foolproof. One plans, learns, reviews and plans further.

One learns three times more from failure than success. One learns three times more clearly when witnessing and analyzing the failures of others they know or have followed. History teaches us about cycles, trends, misapplications of resources, wrong approaches and vacuums of thought. People must apply history to their own lives-situations. If we document our own successes, then these case studies will make us more successful in the future.

Things we do that set us up for failure include:

- Remembering things like they once were...trying to recreate as we believe they were.
- Doing things purely for creative fulfillment...without comprehending the realities.
- Thinking that business acquaintances really care about us as human beings.
- Expecting that others will treat us as fairly as we treat them.
- Hoping that volunteer contributions to the community will be repaid in business referrals.

Fear is the biggest contributor to failure, and it can be a motivator for success. I use FEAR as an acronym for Find Excellence After Reflection. We are just as afraid of the things we don't know as the things in front of us. Most unknown fears turn out to not be as we had imagined.

Opportunists trade and capitalize upon fear. Several professions exist to help people get a grip on their fears. Those trying to sell will tell people what they want to hear or portray the product as being in their best interest. Some people and organizations turn others' fears into propaganda weapons for their own agendas (open or hidden). Some people and organizations take great delight in capitalizing upon the fears of others.

People are most afraid of what they don't understand. If a person scares easily, so will his neighbor. Both can know it, but they're more scared that each other will see it. After awhile, fearful people feel manipulated by others and don't know who to trust.

It is difficult to figure how people will behave when the chips are down. The definition of bravery is a person who is scared but still does what he-she has to.

The Biggest Mistakes Which I Have Made

Personal abilities, talents

- Making the same mistakes more than twice, without studying the mitigating factors.

- Taking incidents out of context and mis-diagnosing situations.

- Rationalizing occurrences, after the fact.

- Appearing self-contained, therefore precluding others from wanting to help me.

- Inability to cultivate other people's support of me at the times that I needed it most.

Resources

- Attempting projects without the proper resources to do the job well.

- Not knowing people with sufficient pull and power. Thinking that friends would help introduce me or help network to key influentials.

- Failure to effective networking techniques early enough in my career path.

- Inability to finely develop the powers of people participating in the networking process.

Other people

- Accepting people at their words without questioning.

- Showing proper respect to other people and assuming that they would show or were capable of showing comparable respect to others.

- Doing favors for others without asking anything in return...if I expected quid pro quo at a later time. Not telling people what I wanted and then being disappointed that they did not read minds or deliver favors of their own volition.

- Befriending people who were too needy...always taking without offering to reciprocate. Continuing to feed their needs...a one-way relationship.

- Picking the wrong causes to champion at the wrong times and with insufficient resources.

- Working with the false assumption that people

want and need comparable things. Incorrectly assuming that all would pursue their agendas fairly. A better understanding of personality types, human motivations and behavioral factors would have provided insight to handle situations on a customized basis.

- Offering highly creative ideas and brain power to those who could not grasp their brilliance...especially to those who were fishing for free ideas they could then market as their own.

Circumstances beyond my control

- Working with equipment, resources and people from a source without my standards of quality control...trying to make the best of bad situations.

- Changing trends, upon which I could not capitalize but which others could.

Mis-calculations

- Incorrectly estimating the time and resources necessary to do something well.

- Getting blindsided because I did not do enough research.

- Failure to plan sufficiently ahead, at the right times.

- Setting sights too low. Not thinking big enough.

Timing

- Offering advice before it was solicited.
- Feeling pressured to offer solutions before diagnosing situations properly.
- Not thinking of enough angles and possibilities...sooner.

Marketplace-external factors

- Not reading the opportunities soon enough.
- Not being able to spot, create or capitalize upon emerging trends at their beginnings.

Stages of mistakes

1. Discovering errors (sensory-motor, sounds-language and logical selection).
2. Recognizing mistakes.
3. Separating successful elements from failures we do not need to duplicate.
4. Learning from mistakes.
5. Learning from success.

6. Mentoring yourself and others toward a higher stream of knowledge.

7. The wisdom that comes from making mistakes, comprehending their outcomes, and developing a knowledge base to achieve success.

Gradations of failing

1. Not seeing the warning signs.

2. Distinguishing among friends, enemies and the majority group, those who could care less about you but who will tap whatever resources available to get their needs met.

3. Never seeing victories as quite enough.

4. Feeling that someone else—everyone else—wins when you fail.

5. Repeating self-defeating behaviors.

6. Holding unrealistic views.

7. Thinking that you never fail...that failing is for other people and organizations.

Gradations of learning from mistakes

1. Distance one's self from one's actions.

2. Become self-critical.

3. Recognize that actions have consequences.

4. Begin accepting responsibility for the consequences.

5. Learn how to eliminate errors.

6. Learn how to learn from mistakes.

7. Accept fallibility, become open to critical feedback and modify actions accordingly.

Gradations of success (i.e. learning from failures)

1. How "Success" is Overrated. Ask various people their definitions of success, and you get many definitions: wealth, power, creativity, leadership, perks, respect, insight, etc. Holding realistic views of success will make you more successful. Unrealistic dreamers set themselves up for failure.

2. Never Stop Paying Dues. Realize that success is earned and is a progression.

3. The In-Between Zone. Getting the most from the ordinary. Learning from every step in between.

4. Put Accurate Labels on Human Transactions. Learn what makes other people tick. Frame situations in a win-win mode. Study behavioral styles.

5. Deal with Fear and Turn it to Your Advantage. Studying the subtleties and sophistications of learning, perceiving and feeling is the mark of maturity. "I failed. Therefore, I learned." Knowledge and perspective equate to success.

6. Continually Shifting and Updating Your Perspectives. How Quickly Things Change. Relish change. Understand how you turn things around.

7. Critical Factors of Success. Study the dynamics of (1) People who just want to get by. (2) Organizations which don't really know why they exist. (3) People who think they're taking short cuts to get riches the fast way. (4) Situations which demand failure before success can be realized. (5) Situations which prevent true success from ever being attained.

Quotes to Ponder

"To do a great right, do a little wrong."
William Shakespeare

"The only one who makes no mistakes is one who never does anything."
Theodore Roosevelt

"A life spent in making mistakes is not more honorable but more useful than a life spent doing nothing."
George Bernard Shaw

"Tis better to have loved and lost than never to have lost at all."

Samuel Butler

"A miss is as good as a mile."

Proverb

"There's no success like failure."

Bob Dylan

"That's life. That's what the people say. You're flying high in April...shot down in May. Each time I find myself flat on my face, I pick myself up and get back in the race. That's life. I can't deny it. I thought of quitting, but my heart ain't gonna buy it."

Frank Sinatra (lyrics to the song, "That's Life," authors D. Kay-K. Gordon) (1966)

"Well, back to the old drawing board."

Peter Arno, 20th Century cartoonist

"The crime is not to avoid failure. The crime is not to give triumph a chance."

Huw Wheldon, 20th Century British broadcaster

"There's a little bit of success in every failure and a little bit of failure in every success."

O. Henry, short story writer

"The only thing we have to fear is fear itself."

Franklin D. Roosevelt (1933)

"Fear has many eyes and can see things underground."

Cervantes, Don Quixote

"You may take the most gallant sailor, the most intrepid airman, or the most audacious soldier. Put them at a table together. What do you get? The sum of their fears."

Winston Churchill

"To fight a bull when you are not scared is nothing. To not fight a bull when you are scared is nothing. But, to fight a bull when you are scared, that is something."

Manolete, bullfighter

"The reasonable man adapts himself to the world. The unreasonable man persists in trying to adapt the world to himself. Therefore, all progress depends on the unreasonable man."

George Bernard Shaw

"We are like dwarves upon the shoulders of giants, and so able to see more and farther than the ancients.

Bernard of Chartres

"People only see what they are prepared to see."

Ralph Waldo Emerson (1863)

"A moment's insight is worth a life's experience."

Oliver Wendell Holmes

"A danger foreseen is half avoided."

Thomas Fuller

"Two men look out through the same bars. One sees the mud, and one the stars."

Frederick Langbridge

7 Benefits Stemming from Failure

1. Immediate Feedback. It is far better to succeed or fail...being stuck in that great middle on uncertainty doesn't give much feedback. Not knowing where we're going or how we're doing causes us to make many more mistakes.

2. Starting Over. When you get the chance to try new things or do things new ways, it serves to re-level the playing field. Without being bogged down by systems and processes that haven't worked, you can create as you go. Starting over is difficult for most people to do. After they've done it, they feel richer for the experience, though knowing of riches on the front end doesn't make starting over any easier.

3. Learn What Not to Do Next Time. Gives you a clear frame of reference, assuming that you clearly understand factors behind the failure, rather than blaming them on someone else.

4. How the Pendulum Swings. One succeeds much more than one fails. By studying swings of the pendulum (likelihoods of failures), one better understands their progress.

5. Failures Make the Best Case Studies. When the facts and fallacies are studied, they are less likely to be replicated in the future. Case studies of success and failure form the basis for training, Strategic Planning, Continuous Quality

Improvement, Visioning, Futurism and other sophisticated business practices.

6. Lessons Learned But Not Soon Forgotten. One learns three times more from failures than success. One succeeds 5-9 times more often than one fails (depending upon the individual's attitude, resources and abilities to develop insights).

7. Qualities of Achievements. The more sophisticated the understanding of failures and their factors, the more successful in business and life the person-organization will be.

15

Mastery of the Big Picture

Trends and Issues Affecting the Future of Business

The business climate ahead is tough and filled with uncertainty, which translates into opportunities. Those who believe the old ways still work shall fall by the wayside. Innovation and the ability to fill new niches will signal the successful businesses of the future.

Take this quick test, as part of your strategic planning for the next two years:

- Does your company have a cohesive business plan, with results-oriented positioning and marketing objectives, updated every year?

- What is the nature of your business now, as compared to when you entered it? What has changed, and who are the new entrants?

- Which marketplace factors are out of your control? Which do your competitors control? Which are within your company's grasp?

- How well does the marketplace understand your organization and its value to the business bottom line? Are there misperceptions that need changing?

- Are you active in professional associations or chambers of commerce? Are they meeting your business needs?

- How much has your company given back to the communities which support you? Is there an organized plan of reciprocation, with a business development design?

- How well trained are your employees? Do they have the company vision? With some fine-tuning, how much could you multiply the effectiveness of your workforce?

The successful manager identifies and meets emerging issues before they take tolls. With informed outside counsel, the manager charts the company's course in a judicious manner.

In an era of downsizing, cutbacks and a reluctance to expand, the same four principles of market dominance are still applicable:

1. Sell new customers. Without adding to the base, the business goes flat.

2. Cross-sell existing customers. They are easier to convince and see great credibility in your company. Most customers do not know all the product-service lines that you offer. It's your obligation to enlighten them, to facilitate their making wise buying choices.

3. Create and market new products-services. Having that mousetrap does not mean that the public will automatically beat a path to your door.

4. Joint-venture to create additional marketplace opportunities. By combining disciplines, you can attract new business and pursue new, creative solutions for clients. We can no longer do business as Lone Rangers.

Trends and Factors Shaping the Future

Categorized per each branch of The Business Tree™

Based upon our studies of the business climate, counseling with top corporations and insight into business problems and challenges, I have identified the major emerging issues of the next two years. These factors will radically open new doors for those companies which are prepared.

1. The business you're in
   Results-driven business.
   Competition and changing marketplaces.
   Deregulations.
   Industry segments.

2. Running the business
   Downsizing.
   Technologies.
   Business conducted at home.
   Creating new efficiencies.
   Rules, responsibilities and ethics.

3. Financial
   Fluctuating economies.
   Global economic development.
   Incomes of companies vs. earnings.

4. People
   Workplace illiteracy.
   Societal changes.
   Consequences to changing cultural panorama.
   Workforce diversity.
   Generational differences.
   Drug testing (deemed legal in court challenges).
   Age discrimination.
   Back-handed ethnic discrimination, detriments to diversity.
   Perceptions of a homogenous workforce.
   Education of the workforce.

5. Business development
   Branding and niche marketing.
   Cause Related Marketing.

6. Body of Knowledge
   Intellectual property issues.
   Fear, failure and success ratios.
   External influencers.
   Regulators and Government Relations.

7. The Big Picture
   Growing necessity for longterm strategy.
   Strategic repositioning.
   Corporate Cultures.

7 Biggest Misconceptions About Business

1. Winning is paramount...no matter what the prize. Prove that you're right by making others wrong. It's not enough to win, but the competitors should suffer. "Might makes right" mentality blurs reasonable decisions by business leaders.

2. Executives know what they are doing. They are properly trained and have all resources necessary to manage. Belief that executives have all talents, especially people skills. This puts company destiny in the hands of people who themselves need to be groomed-mentored.

3. Employees are sufficiently trained to do their jobs. They are college educated...so what more do they need? Policies and procedures will take care of everything else. Employees know what they should do. Professional development is a waste of money. This mindset leads to mis-use, mis-casting and costly make-goods by the company's most valuable resource, its people.

4. Technology and gadgets make the extra difference. Technology will solve all company

problems. Besides, putting money into gadgets means that you don't have to address other shortcomings. People tend to focus more upon gadgetry than deeper organizational issues.

5. Flaws can be excused, patched or scapegoated elsewhere. If sales are up, then the company must be "doing something right." Temporary success excuses company dysfunction. Artificial success is the downfall of every organization.

6. Customers' opinions don't matter as much as that of the CEO. Don't ask for substantive input, nor evaluate what is uncovered. Efforts directed toward making the company policies right and, therefore, the customer wrong. This sabotages business development.

7. That there really is a master plan. More often, the "plan" is a series of sales projections-quotas and says that problems will be handled via "band aid surgery," only at such time as it is absolutely necessary. It's amazing how many companies rigidly refer to "plans" that don't really exist.

Fads, Panaceas and Quick Fixes Utilized by Businesses Rather than Focus Upon and Plan for the Big Picture

Activity-based costing
After-action review

Agile manufacturing
Benchmarking
Branding
Cognitive therapy
Commitment management
Continuous improvement & TQM processes
Core competencies
Customer focus
Cycle-time reduction
Dialog decision process
Downsizing--Rightsizing
Economic value-added
Groupware
Information technology architecture & systems
Learning organizations
Outsourcing
Process engineering
Scenario planning
Self-directed teams
Sense and respond
Skill sets
Strategic alliances
System dynamics
Total quality management
Value chain analysis

Problems and Challenges Facing Growing Companies

Progress vs. isolationism. For all we have achieved, our society is more polarized than ever. Like minds and appearances surround themselves with those like themselves. Diversity is not sought. Sameness is the mantra, by default.

Focus on micro vs. macro. It's easy and convenient to zero in on small details than to solve problems...than to get at root causes of deeper issues. Very few managers have ever been taught to become skilled generalists. Big Picture thinking is not given much of a forum.

Band-Aid surgery for all business problems. Society is predicated upon putting out the latest "fire," only when it arises. Most businesses deny the existence of a Big Picture and cannot plan for it. They don't utilize strategic planning and visioning processes because they were never taught any, nor know what they are. Thus, band-aid surgery costs businesses six times more each year than the broader approach which this book advocates.

Workplace illiteracy. Half of the corporate workforce is functionally illiterate, making costly decisions and failing to conserve company resources. They may have degrees and computer savvy, but thinking-reasoning skills, people experiences and professionalism have not been developed. The common denominator of today's workforce is lower than it was 25 years ago. Workplace illiteracy is at an all-time high. Educated people are making costly mistakes in business, and their supervisors are not comprehending the reasons why. Continuous quality improvement can and should be effected.

Poor and nonexistent customer service. Customer service is presently at an all-time low...and getting worse. Business does not comprehend how it poorly treats, mistreats or neglects its means of support. We must always make the customer a priority. Customer service is something that we think and do, not an add-on sale. It must be inculcated into every dynamic of business, at every level in the organization and with accountability factors attached.

Technology overload and overexcuse. Tech-nology is wonderful, yet it represents a fraction of a percent of organizational importance. In 1999, business spent $600 billion on Y2K compliance...diverting funds from planning, training, marketplace development and other priority issues. At least it was a form of planning, though proper front-end visioning would have precluded Y2K expenditures. Technology gets unfairly blamed and scapegoated for problems in other areas of the organization, becoming a barrier to customer service. More people have computer skills than people skills. We must utilize technology as the wonderful machinery that it is...but not let it preclude wholistic development of the business.

The high cost of hype. Some companies believe the statements that they are issuing. Some either skillfully lie to get what they think they want...or may really believe themselves to be what they hype to publics who don't know any better. Many consumers are gullible, "name" crazy and susceptible to grandiose claims. They take what is said at face value because they have not or don't care to develop abilities to discern what is hyped by others. They believe distortions faster than they believe facts, logic and reason. Consumers naively believe mis-representations...to the exclusion of organizations which are more conservative, yet substantive, in their informational offerings.

Further spinning. People talk and perceive life in "spin doctor" bites, rather than true perceptions. This comes from teasers on TV newscasts, which lead to incorrect generalizations, which lead to patterns of thinking. Politicians and purposefully-nebulous business leaders put more sophisticated "spins" on the same concepts. Thus, the average person in the street emulates these patterns of talking, which become their methodologies for viewing life, which cloud objective thinking.

Button-pushing society. We want quick fixes, which usually lead to bills of goods that someone is selling. Our society continually seeks button-pushing answers for life's complex problems without paying enough dues toward a truly successful life. This book is the antithesis to that phenomenon...showing that business is an array of ideologies, processes and subtle nuances. Avoiding the temptation to short-circuit the necessary steps is really the road to gold.

Shoot, ignore or ostracize the messenger. Most advice is obtained from the wrong consultants. Companies buy bills of goods from people who recommend what they're selling, rather than what is really needed. Thus, consultants are scapegoated and given a bad name. Blaming someone else is a way of avoiding the processes of improvement and quality.

Putting tomorrow in someone else's hands. Tomorrow is ours to craft, not that of vendors. Futurism is a process of thinking, reasoning, creative problem solving, interaction with others, thinking outside your frame of reference and personal commitment. Futurism is not esoteric, nor is it a quick fix. It is a process of change, 90% beneficial.

Opportunities and Positive Factors

Workforce diversity. We do not look the same anymore, nor should we. Ethnic, cultural and societal differences should be studied and understood by management. Issues of age and handicap status should be addressed in a pro-active manner.

Global economic development. Long before free trade agreements, NAFTA or the internet, we were a global economy. Hiding our heads in the sand or pretending to think global while really behaving myopically will bury us. Open and cultivate new markets.

Downsizing. People who were formerly employed in the corporate world need retraining to function in an entrepreneurial environment.

Outsourcing and privatization. It makes good sense to utilize the most efficient resources. No company can or should have all the resources. It is cost-effective and stimulating to the business to outsource services, lease employees, offer alternate worksite options, joint-venture with other companies for shared services and create other ways of doing business better, faster and cheaper. Corporations need to be trained on effective use of outsourcing. Privatization of services needs to rise to a new plateau.

Collaborating, partnering and joint-venturing. Put three parts together and come up with a five-edged arsenal. Matching disciplines (complimentary or non-traditional) will create endless opportunities and give marketplace advantage. Chapter 7 in this book is devoted exclusively to this topic. Few companies have explored this area yet...most will have to do it in order to adapt to the future.

Generational differences. Though not exposed to the values, work ethic and experiences of older but wiser generations, today's workforce has a wealth of opportunities. The objective is to avoid taking the quick-fix and flash-and-sizzle routes. By combining the best of the old and the new, the next business generations will be far more successful.

Strategic repositioning. Companies must utilize objective outside professionals to detect problems, create opportunities and monitor that evolution takes place. The worst mistake is thinking that you've got it all under control...that kind of mindset festers until the organization stagnates permanently.

Branding and niche marketing. Not everyone is your customer. First, determine who your market niche is not. That will save countless wasted energies. By studying why some customers are not your likely target, this will help streamline the short list of likeliest customer niches.

Cause related marketing. Unless a company gives back to the community, it has no right to be in business. The skill of determining applicable, business-oriented philanthropic objectives requires careful thought and reaps countless rewards for the well-intentioned organization.

Team building. People are your organization's most valuable commodity. Reduce wasted effort by empowering employees. Encourage training, professional development, service in professional associations and community involvement. Employees work better when they think highly of their company and vice versa.

Ethics. Prepare and distribute a company ethics statement. The process will dramatically bolster your company, if conducted properly.

Government relations. Be sure that you understand and maintain effective relationships with public officials, regulatory agencies and other public sector entities which could hurt or help your business. Communicate with them before you need something. Become a credible resource of expert opinion, not just a special interest.

Management Challenges, Opportunities for the Future of Business

Categorized per each branch of The Business Tree™

1. The business you're in
   Delivery of products and services.
   Fewer safety nets, less reliance upon the old ways.

2. Running the business
   Productivity through uncertainty.
   Putting technology into perspective.
   Quality.

3. Financial
   Economies without borders.
   Outsourcing and privatization.
   Accountability, measurements and benchmarking.

4. People
   Feminization and diversification of organizational culture.
   Team building and team links.
   Professional education, development and training.
   Communications and trust.

Rights and respect.
Awards, incentives and recognition.
Performance reviews.
Personal visions and plans...employee ownership of their productivity and, thus, the company.
Problem-solving skills.

5. Business development
   Methods of communications.
   Customer relations. Providing value-added.
   E-business and debunking the e-business myths.
   Research....Human Intelligence.
   Court of public opinion.

6. Body of Knowledge
   Collaborating, Partnering and Joint-Venturing.
   Front-burner business issues.
   Institutionalization of rapid change.
   New understanding of organizations.
   Growth strategies programs.
   Crisis management and preparedness.
   Executive leadership. Mentoring heir apparents and future executives.
   Cooperations with government and the private sector.
   Champions, inspirors and visionaries.

7. The Big Picture
   Worldwide competition for new ideas.
   Creative idea generation.
   Strategies and stages in management implementation.
   Strategic Planning and Corporate Visioning.

Factors of Futurism Which Must Be Addressed

New kinds of products
A new company
The past as a teaching tool
Retreading old knowledge, technologies, marketing and products
Necessities
Changing competition
Turning competitors into collaborators and some-time-suppliers
Putting people above technology
Customer focus
The customer's customer
Information overhead...cutting through the clutter
Changing definitions of productivity
Where new ideas come from
Creating new business concepts, philosophies, processes
Levels of understanding
Developing insights-visions beyond information
Concurrent Re-Engineering
Thinking Ahead
Crisis Management and Preparedness
Taking Futurism Out of the Esoteric and into Daily Utilization
The past as a teaching tool
See how far you've come.
Continue to benchmark and recognize progress.
See what things that you could not do before this process began.
End goals are not the objective...making strides is most important.
Recognize that no end goal may be reached.

Goals are constantly changing.
Create a "buddy system," a network of supporters for your pro-active process.
Change in realistic increments.

Top 21st Century Futures

1. E-Cybernation: Computers, TV, newspapers, and other media merge, along with their content--entertainment, news, training, etc.

2. Bio-Age: Biotechnology transforms medicine, eliminating many human ills.

3. Personal Robot Slaves: Sentient but obedient robots will become affordable and commonplace.

4. Intelligent Things: Computer chips will be embedded in all of our stuff--and in ourselves.

5. Exploiting Outer Space: Exploration of our neighboring planets will lead to settling, mining, and manufacturing.

6. Quantum, Nanotech, and Holodeck Computer Ages: Computers are destined to become a billion times more capable than today's systems.

7. Interactive TV Shows: The entertainment industry will continue to be a key driver of technological advances.

8. Nonlethal Weapons: Public safety will increase

thanks to advances in humane crime fighting and weapons technologies.

9. Redesigned Humans: Bioengineering will merge with computing to create healthier, wiser people.

10. Doubling of Human Life-Spans: Reversing the physical and mental processes of aging may soon be within our reach.

7 Ingredients of Success

1. Finding knowledge in new and unique ways. Strive to learn something new everyday. Learn from examples (good and bad). Education leads to knowledge, which leads to wisdom. Develop continuing education, professional development and life philosophies.

2. Doing work that you're proud of. No matter what the job title, task or career orientation, work can be done professionally. If it doesn't mean something to you, it will not contribute to the marketplace or society at large. When you value it, they will begin to reciprocate.

3. Developing a philosophy...individually and organizationally. Analyze where you've been. Evaluate strengths and weaknesses. Analyze and strategize opportunities. Establish bigger goals this year than you had last year...with means and reasons for reaching them.

4. Handling mistakes and crises. Everyone makes mistakes. The mark of Quality is how you handle them. Learn the art of diagnosing problems, taking input and effecting workable solutions. Planning for crises will divert them from occurring, 85% of the time. Waiting until the last moment to apply "band-aid surgery" is self-defeating and costly.

5. Dealing with fear. Everyone has fear. Those who deny it the most are detrimental to your success and that of your organization. Understand fears, and set plans to work with them. Remove barriers to success. Turn internal fears into motivating forces. Fears will never go away...but can facilitate the path toward success.

6. Learning to read others' screens. Put yourself in other people's shoes, and communicate in their sphere...to achieve desired actions-results. Learn what motivates others and colors their take on life...in order to work well with diverse peoples and organizational cultures.

7. Self fulfillment, purpose and commitment. Career-Life Vision, Body of Work. Develop a strategic plan, core values and action steps to accomplish your dreams. While others may roam aimlessly through life, you will achieve, sustain and share success. Commit to and thrive on change.

Advice to Management

Charting the course of a company is a lofty responsibility, with so many factors riding on the outcome. It's lonely at the top, and most corporate executives are hard pressed to know where to turn for informed opinion. Effectively utilize outside advisors.

Having consulted and implemented programs in all of the above-listed areas for corporate, public sector and mid-sized business clients, we have quantified the efficiencies of front-end investment.

Longterm planning facilitates a total and cohesive business approach. It signals the future and new, creative ways of doing things. Think to the future, and analyze where your company wishes to be. With strategic planning and implementation, success is attainable.

16

The Court of Public Opinion

It's not enough to simply make a good widget. Every organization must be in the widget production, distribution, marketing, selling and deliverability business.

Fundamental to running a successful business is the necessity to craft, fine-tune, perpetuate, benchmark and evolve the organization's image, public posture and the intricately subtle nuances of same. Corporate communications does not just happen all by itself. It must reflect careful forethought toward a changing corporate culture, with layers of sophisticated actions in congruity with that culture.

All too often, service providers within various niches of the communications specialty fields are called upon. The result is a patchwork of conflicting images, rather than a tapestry of what best suits the organization. Often, organizational communications image is biased by the slant of the service provider quilt currently being used for cover.

How organizations start out and what they become are different concepts. Mistakes, niche orientation and lack of planning lead businesses to failure. Processes, trends, fads, perceived stresses and "the system" force managers to make compromises in order to proceed. Often, a fresh look at previous knowledge gives renewed insight.

The purpose of "The Court of Public Opinion" is to encompass corporate communications under one umbrella. Underlying tenets for the organization that should be followed through the communications program include:

- Think Big Picture.
- Conceptualize and communicate your company's own goals.
- Understand conflicting societal goals.
- Fit your dreams into the necessities and realities of the real world.
- Find your own niche...do your thing.
- Get satisfactions from doing something well and committing to long-term excellence.
- Seek truths in unusual and unexpected sources.
- Share your knowledge, and learn further by virtue of mentoring others.

In many industries and professions, business development has occurred primarily by accident or through market demand. Because of economic realities and the increased numbers of firms providing comparable services, the notion of business development is now a necessity, rather than a luxury. Competition for customers-clients is sharpening. The professions are no longer held on a pedestal...a condition which mandates them to portray or enhance public images.

As companies adjust comfort levels and acquire confidence in the arena of business development, there is a direct relationship of the success of corporate communications to billings, client mix diversity, market share, competitive advantage, stock price and levels of business which enable other planned growth.

Public perceptions are called "credence goods" by economists. Every organization must educate outside publics about what they do and how they do it. This premise also holds true for each corporate operating unit and department. The whole of the business and each sub-set must always educate corporate opinion makers on how it functions and the skill with which the company operates.

Gaining confidence among stakeholders is crucial. Business relationships with customers, collaborators and other professionals are established to be long-term in duration. Each organization should determine and craft its own corporate culture, character and personality, seeking to differentiate itself from others.

Top management must endorse corporate communications, if your company is to grow and prosper. Few companies can even sustain present levels of sales without some degree of business development.

Some people in your organization will devote much time to promotions, public relations, marketing and advertising. This quality should be recognized and rewarded...since professionals with a sense of business direction play an important part in company growth. Be it a "necessary evil" or not, corporate imaging activity can be accomplished with skill and success.

The professional organization that evokes a consistent image—and backs it up with actions—will prosper in today's rapidly changing marketplace. In image building, the following ideas should be considered:

- Your company and profession fill essential needs of society.
- Each key staff member represents a learned profession.
- Qualities denoting your company include skill, expertise, objectivity and independence.
- Work and abilities of your employees are diverse and creative.
- Your key management team is dynamic, in terms of business issues.
- The marketplace is rapidly expanding and is an excellent career choice for young people.
- Your team encompasses multi-dimensional professionals...concerned with much more than the immediate responsibilities of the work at hand.
- Recognize the role of professional communicators. Seek qualified counsel.

Essential Ingredients of a Corporate Communications Program

The organization's Visioning Program takes years to

develop. It is a hybrid of strategic planning, corporate culture, benchmarks and the dreams of the company. It must embrace top-down and bottom-up support. Producing the Visioning Program requires teamwork from across the organization. Frequent communications about the program's progress may be the arena for qualified communications professionals.

For public companies, a format Investor Relations Program has direct relationship to book value on Wall Street, stock price, stakeholder confidence and applicability toward long-term growth. Its writing and maintenance must encompass professionals from the planning, financial and communications disciplines, working together as a company brain trust.

Every organization must have a formal, written, sustainable and measurable Public Relations Program. Its components should include complete generic press kits, guidelines on working with the media and pointers on training staff as media spokespersons. It should also encompass the company's collateral literature system, guidelines on arranging speeches, seminars and town hall meetings and ways to improve local community and government relations.

The Marketing Program should include sales support, business development, direct marketing, indirect marketing, advertising, business-to-business promotions, industry and professional marketing, point-of-purchase materials and collateral materials.

Every corporation must have a formal written Communications Manual. This is utilized by all departments and standardizes the overall communications philosophy. It establishes writing style and subject areas of statements to make publicly. It should also set corporate precedence for letters, forms, customer comment cards, customer service correspondence, sales manuals and graphics standards.

There should exist a Crisis Management and Preparedness Plan. This embodies "what if" scenario planning and addresses contingencies which the organization will take in times of specified and unplanned emergencies.

Literature and audio visual programs portray the company image, which must be consistent and cohesive. So do the Special Financial Publics program, government relations program, community relations program, corporate philanthropy program and professional enhancement program.

Corporate Communications should also be involved and incorporated in essential documents and programs which are generated by other departments. These include the company's Strategic Plan, Policies and Procedures, internal auditing and assessment program, compensation, benefits, financial plans, accounts payable-receivable plans, conflict resolution-arbitration plans, the Continuous Quality Improvement program, the organizational Ethics Statement, job Descriptions and staff training programs.

What Corporate Communications Accomplishes

A well planned, reasonable and diverse program should have many noble goals. With implementation by communications professionals and embracement by all strata of the organization, the expected accomplishments may include:

- Prestige or favorable image...and its benefits.

- Promotions of products and sales.

- Goodwill of the employees.
- Prevention and solution of labor problems.
- Fostering the goodwill of communities in which the company has units.
- Goodwill of the stockholders, board of directors, and owners.
- Overcoming misconceptions and prejudices.
- Goodwill of suppliers.
- Goodwill of government.
- Goodwill of the rest of your industry.
- Attraction of others into the industry.
- Ability to attract the best personnel.
- Education of the public to the purposes and scope of the product.
- Education of the public to a point of view.
- Good will of customers (and their friends and colleagues).
- Seeing that the industry is properly represented in the curricula of schools and colleges, by assisting educators in teaching about the industry.

- Creating public support for legislative proposals that the industry favors or public opposition to legislation that it opposes.

- Obtaining public recognition for the social and economic contributions that the industry makes to the nation.

- Combatting government interference or competition with the industry.

- Public understanding of the regulation of the industry by the government, in order to assure equitable regulation.

- Consumer understanding of how to use the product.

We expect that an ongoing corporate communications program should affect these viewpoints by the public:

- Your service is efficient and excellent, by your standards and by the publics. You are sensitive to the public's needs, and you are flexible and human in meeting them.

- Your staff is likeable and competent. They demonstrate initiative and use their best judgment, with authority to make the decisions they should make.

- You have a good reputation and are awake to community obligations. You contribute much to the economy. You provide leadership for progress, rather than following along.

- You always give your customers their money's worth. Your charges are fair and reasonable. You employ state-of-the-art technology and are in the vanguard of your industry.

- You provide a good place to work. You offer a promising career and future for people with ideas and initiative. Your people do a day's work for a day's pay.

- The size of your organization is necessary to do the job demanded of you. Your integrity and dependability make the public confident that you will use your size and influence rightly.

17

Since September 11

Defining Moments in the Corporate Culture
Crisis Management as a Planning Tool

Every business and community in America is presently at a crossroads. The events of September 11, 2001, may generally be seen as a beacon for planning, reflection and optimistic venturing toward the future.

There exist two current options for businesses in the much-publicized post-September 11th time frames:

1. Each organization can be seen and known as a dynamic community that addresses its problems and moves forward in a heroic fashion...as a role model to the rest of the world.

2. Or, organizations can bury their heads in the sand and hope media attention dies down...thus becom-

ing a generic tagline for troubled business waters.

Certainly, all of us want to choose option one and seek complex answers for the judicious practices of moving forward.

Volatile business contractions, uneasy economic climate, plant explosions, health care crises, hostile corporate takeovers, governmental shakeups, and financial failings are crises that upset the routine of business life.

These occurrences or their variations are feared by the business community. Some jolting incident puts every organization into a reaction mode. The consequences of miscommunication in a crisis can be devastating to all involved.

By dealing with the unexpected, preferably before it occurs, companies can bank public goodwill that may be useful later. Playing catch-up means that you have lost the game.

Among the types of crises that I have advised clients include government reorganizations, plant explosions, contaminated food and drugs, school shootings, executive kidnappings, installation bombings, hostile company takeovers, natural disasters and problematic employee behaviors. In doing so, I have learned that strategic planning for crises can avert them 85% of the time. In times of crisis, business does what it should have done earlier: study, reflect, plan and manage change.

It is the responsibility of corporate management to practice effective Crisis Management and Preparedness. Management must study practical experiences of what can go wrong, put a crisis team into place, understand the workings of news media, identify community opinion leaders, and predict potentially harmful or controversial situations.

Comprehension of the dangers includes case studies of how other corporations handled emergencies. Learn from those who were successful, those who failed to achieve the desired effects, and those whose corporate credibilities were damaged by doing nothing.

Planning for Crises

I recommend that every organization take the following courses of action:

First, establish a committee to write, implement and benchmark a formal Crisis Management and Preparedness Plan. Its contents should include a mechanism for determining potential crises, identification of audiences to be effected and procedures to follow during a crisis. There should be contingency plans to facilitate routine business during crisis, selection and training of a crisis management team and coordination of what information can and cannot be released. Once written and tailored for organizational needs, the plan must be discussed and understood at all levels within the company.

Second, try to defuse disasters, confrontations, loss of public credibility and decreased ability to do future business by investigating steps that might prevent crises, establishing adequate standby measures and formulating a followup program to recoup the company's good name. Follow through with significant community relations activities to bank goodwill.

Third, make provisions, policies and processes for interfacing with news media. They should include a list of emergency phone numbers, available to the media, designated work areas for media and an internal hotline number for media, as well as a separate hotline for the public.

Take assessment of damages, and investigate the truth. Never exaggerate, speculate, or withhold information. No statements should be "off the record." Provide complete answers, and respond to media requests for additional information in a timely manner. Failure to return calls implies something to hide. Maintain accurate records of all inquiries and news coverage.

During any emergency, utilize these rules for communications: State the issues. Define problem areas. Identify the issues. Move forward.

Fourth, during crisis situations, there must be one designated spokesperson with enough credibility and command of information to present the company image. Guard against the fact that, sometimes, the spokesperson becomes the negative focus of the story...not the message itself. When a company makes a statement, it plays off the history of past statements. If a reverse stand is taken, then the company must provide a plausible explanation. Media will rarely change its position after the fact.

The selection and training of spokespersons is a judgment call by corporate management and public relations professionals. Extensive training must be conducted on media presentation skills, message points, speeches to non-media audiences, followup written communications and community positioning. It's more than just looking good before a camera.

Fifth, test crisis plans during simulated drills, using qualified outside strategic planning consultants to evaluate results. Company officials should take these simulations seriously. The military does, terming them "war games."

Sixth, part of being prepared is routine activity. Have a plan in force (with the added benefit of legal counsel), and be sure that every employee has a copy. It should include easy-to-read fact sheets and backgrounders on company operations, current phone numbers, and a delineated line of authority (from company resource people to the spokesperson)

Seventh, recognize new and different crises in the making. Elements that prevent most companies from predating crises include:

- Ignorance of the information.
- Making of incorrect assumptions about the opposition.
- Bad judgment by failure to get objective information and lack of planning.
- Failure to communicate your story via all levels of line staff.

What Causes Crises?

Crises can have many liabilities upon companies, including loss of profits and market share. Inevitable spin-offs include government investigations, public scrutiny, and a tarnished image. This causes loss of employee morale and, as a result, company productivity.

Based upon research and experience with hundreds of client situations, I have found that seven types of crises exist:

1. Those Resulting from Doing Nothing. The biggest problem with business, in a one-sentence capsule: People exhibit misplaced priorities and impatience...seeking profit and power, possess-

ing unrealistic views of life, and not fully willing to do the things necessary to sustain orderly growth and long-term success.

2. Doing Things as We Always Have. Resulting from inflexible conditions, obsolete policies-procedures, procrastination, attitude, resistance to innovation, failure to change.

3. Those We Bring Upon Ourselves. Don't have sufficient management skills or resources to do something well. Ignore small problems when they occur. Won't listen to advice.

4. Circumstances Beyond Our Control. Miscalculations, manmade disasters, natural disasters, shifting resources, changing marketplaces, regulations, bureaucracies.

5. Bad Work, Poor Planning. Damage control for what someone else did wrong, sub-standard, behind schedule, in poor taste, without regard for quality or ill-prepared.

6. Averted. 85% of the time, planning and forethought will avert the crisis. So, why don't organizations and individuals remediate trouble by planning on the front end?

7. Intervention. Getting past the current crisis does no good unless you take steps to assure that it does not recur. Planning is necessary to remediate current and future problems.

Crisis management and preparedness can minimize negative impacts of any emergency. Going through the planning and implementation is a quality assurance process that strengthens any company. Crisis communications means banking goodwill for those times when the plan is called to the test.

Crises are caused by:

1. Refusal to take action.

2. Letting problems fester until they become epidemic diseases.

3. Lack of accountability.

4. Waiting until it is too late to avert crisis.

5. Taking correctional measures after too much damage has been done.

6. Waiting too late to make good for damage. Saying you're sorry isn't enough.

7. Living life for the moment, without understanding the implications and repercussions.

Crises of one sort can and will happen to every company. They can be turned from disasters into opportunities to project corporate strengths.

The manner in which a crisis is handled often wins praise for companies whose positions are improved in the public eye. Those who are prepared will survive and thrive.

Moments of Truth

There comes a point when the pieces fit. One becomes fully actualized and is able to approach their life's Body of Work. That moment comes after years of trial and error, experiences, insights, successes and failures.

Young people in the workforce sometimes think that they can "have it all" overnight. They don't know how much they don't know. Many aren't willing to pay sufficient dues to "get there."

As one matures, survives, life becomes a giant reflection. We appreciate the journey because we understand it much better. We know where we've gone because we know the twists and turns in the road there. Nobody, including ourselves, could have predicted every curve along the way.

However, some basic tenets charted our course. To understand those tenets is to make full value out of the years ahead. The best is usually yet to come.

Your individual and organizational output should be greater than the sum of your inputs. This is accomplished by reviewing the lessons of life, their contexts, their significances, their accountabilities, their shortcomings and their path in charting your future.

Alas, all of us practice Futurism to some extent. Futurism is not an esoteric concept. It is a potpourri of where we've been, why we've done well and what we're going to do about the lessons learned. That's the common-sense approach to Futurism.

The 7 R's of September 11th

Major crises cause individuals and institutions to profoundly study, plan and vision toward the future. The first time that I wrote such an essay as this was after another date that changed history, November 22, 1963. There have been many others since then...usually in reports to organizations in analysis of their own crises.

I propose that business will emerge stronger and more determined by observing the 7 R's of September 11th: re-examine, reconnect, remediate, resolve, replenish, reform and refocus.

Re-examine. Look at the good in your organization, as well as the areas for improvement. Find the nuggets of wisdom within your own company. Their thinkers will take the whole of the organization to the next tier.

Reconnect. As we do during holidays, family reunions and graduations, reconnect with business partners and resources who got your company to where it is today. Rekindling collaborations with fresh focus will impact your operation.

Remediate. Don't wait for all six coins to stack up. Don't take the same band-aid surgery approaches that ultimately exaggerated the business crisis. Nobody does things perfect on the front end. Remediate the high costs as you go...a process that sparks of planning creativity.

Resolve. This word has been widely reintroduced into the world's vocabulary. Prior to September 11th, Resolve was better known as the name of a carpet cleaner. Resolve is both a noun (purpose, determination) and a verb (change, analyze, deal with successfully, make progress from dissonance). When a person adds "resolve" to his-her active vocabulary, then so do organizations, which are collections of committed people.

Replenish. Performing band-aid surgery on some parts of the organization take their tolls in other areas. During budget crises, vital programs such as training, planning and leadership development get put on the back burner. Actually, it's times of crisis when those burners should be reheated.

Reform. As we study what works successfully, we take honest looks at problematic areas. By making routine modifications to policies and procedures, we reform the problems and inspire the new order.

Refocus. After any crisis, happening, event or action, there will always be a new order. Benefit from change (which is 90% positive), rather than become the victim of it.

Conclusions from Previous Chapters

1. Steps Toward Building Better Business. Painting a Big Picture of business establishes criteria for operating more effectively...thus eliminating the need for so much band-aid surgery.

2. The Path from Pleasure to Success. The manner in which one navigates through the rocky times and takes pro-active steps to recovering from inevitable setbacks speaks toward long-term success. Taking shortcuts will actually deter the journey toward success.

3. The High Cost of Doing Nothing™ . It costs six times more to clean up, react to and recover from mistakes than to do things right on the front end. Human beings are not perfect and don't do everything according to advance planning, though we can develop expeditious ways to remediate damages before the highest costs stack up.

9. Collaborations, Partnering and Joint-Venturing...the

Fastest-Emerging Priority for Business. By establishing new ways of working together, we paint new horizons for organizational success, individually and collectively.

10. You've Got to Be Taught. Plan for training which your organization needs, rather than what training vendors have to sell.

11. Lessons Learned But Not Soon Forgotten. Creative approaches toward problem solving, dealing with business realities and strategic planning in order for organizations to truly succeed exist within each of us.

12. Oxymorons. The more we understand the differences and how people mis-use terms, the more precise we can be about the ingredients of success.

13. The Book of Acronyms. Redefining business terms by what they potentially represent when one looks creatively to expand the scope of their organization. Such thinking results in created opportunities and optimized profitability.

14. The Fine Art of Failure. We must learn from the mistakes of ourselves and others in order to create a more successful business. Without this learning curve, we are destined to make more mistakes and derail the success that the organization has earned.

15. Mastery of the Big Picture. By spotting trends

> beyond the obvious ones and in contexts which we might not otherwise have considered, we take creative steps and assure a better ruin of business success.

The process of planning for the future and moving judiciously forward is a concept called Visioning. Many cities have undergone Visioning programs. Through the process, they experienced citizen input, corporate support, new levels of awareness and attitude shifts. Communities have futures and must plan for them...rather than becoming the victims of someone else's changes.

Visioning is the process where good ideas become something more. Visioning is a catalyst toward long-term evaluation, planning and implementation. Visioning is a jumpoff point by which forward-thinking organizations ask: What will we look like in the future? What do we want to become? How will we evolve? Vision is a realistic picture of what is possible.

Elements for survival and ultimate success include a team orientation, mentorship, access to authority figures, self-esteem of each employee, commitment to the organization and an encouragement to innovate.

Organizations will succeed by having, communicating and garnering support for a Shared Vision. Visioning sets the stage for necessary processes, such as growth strategies, re-engineering, training, enhancing shareholder value and organizational development. Without visioning, the company simply performs band-aid surgery on problems as they occur.

18

Business Partnerships

Essays Affecting the Future of Business Planning Lessons Learned from Y2K

The U.S. economy spent between $800 billion and one trillion dollars fixing and treating the so-called Y2K Bug. Certainly, aspects of the bug were treated successfully, and troubles were averted because of professional actions. No doubt, public hype contributed to a "sky is falling" situation that made computer consultants rich.

Technology constitutes less than 1% of any organization's overall Big Picture. Computer activity constitutes less than 1% of the technology picture. Thus, efforts to treat a fraction of one percent took resources away from addressing the other 99.999% of companies' full-scope planning.

My concern over that three-year period was that money was diverted from most other aspects of organizational wellness toward treating one symptom of one disease. I advocated a balanced approach toward planning, visioning and the Big Picture....I still do.

Rather than bash those who neglected other aspects of the organization in favor of Y2K Readiness, let's refocus what we did and learned toward other future applications.

Among the lessons which we learned from the Y2K Bug exercise were:

- When they want to do so, company leadership will provide sufficient resources to plan for the future, including crisis management and preparedness (of which computer glitches are one set of "what if's.")

- When they want to do so, company leadership will provide leadership for change management and re-engineering...two of the many worthwhile concepts that should be advocated every business day.

- People are the company's most valuable resource, representing 28% of the Big Picture. Today's work force will need three times the amount of training that it presently gets in order for the organization to be competitive in the millennium.

- Change is good. Like change...don't fear it. Change is 90% positive. Without always noticing it, individuals and organizations change 71% per year. The secret is to benefit from change, rather than become a victim of it.

- Pro-active change involves the entire organization. When all departments are consulted and participate in the decisions, then the company is empowered.

- Fear and failure are beneficial too. One learns three times more from failure than from success. Failures propel us toward our greatest future successes.

- When we work with other companies and the public sector, we collaborate better. All benefit, learn from each other and prepare collectively for the future.

- In the future and in order to successfully take advantage of the future, make planning a priority...not a knee-jerk reaction.

Business Mentoring

Coaching industries are growing rapidly because self-styled experts are creating pockets of business for themselves. Demands have long existed for quality service...with few seasoned business advisors available. Thus, niche consultants served the business.

New generations of entry-level consultants are hanging out shingles as "coaches" without backgrounds in guiding people, organizations and processes. Most business coaches used to be something else and are turning to "coaching" in their downsized career period.

Training programs for coaches are available, some good and some nothing more than multi-level marketing. There's presently more marketing to the concept of business coaching than substantive track record.

The hot new idea is to focus on depth-and-substance...not on flash-and-sizzle. Those who proclaim that hot ideas make good coaches, then they are vendors selling flavors of the month...not seasoned business advisors. If coaching is based only on hot ideas, it is nothing more than hucksterism. Coaching must be a thorough process of guiding the client through the levels of accomplishment.

There are 7 Levels at Which Mentors Are Utilized:

1. Resource. Equipment, tools, materials, schedules.

2. Skills and Tasks. Duties, activities, tasks, behaviors, attitudes, contracting, project fulfillment.

3. Role and Job. Assignments, responsibilities, functions, relationships, follow-through, accountability.

4. Systems and Processes. Structure, hiring, control, work design, supervision, decisions.

5. Strategy. Planning, tactics, organizational development.

6. Culture and Mission. Values, customs, beliefs, goals, objectives, benchmarking.

7. Philosophy. Organizational purpose, vision, quality of life, ethics, long-term growth.

There are 7 Levels of business and organizational mentoring:

1. Conveying Information. Initial exposure to the coaching process. One-time meeting or conference between mentors and mentees. The coach is a resource for business trends, societal issues, opportunities. The coach is active listener, coaches on values, actions.

2. Imparting Experiences. The coach becomes a role model. Insight offered about own life-career. Reflection strengthens the mentor and shows mentee levels of thinking and perception which were not previously available to the mentee.

3. Encouraging Actions. The coach is an advocate for progress, change. Empowers the mentee to hear, accept, believe and get results. Sharing of feelings, trust, ideas, philosophies.

4. Paving the Way. The coach endorses the mentee...wants his-her success. Messages ways to approach issues, paths in life to take. Helps draw distinctions. Paints picture of success.

5. Wanting the Best. Continuing relationship between the coach and mentee. Progress is visioned, contextualized, seeded, bench-

marked. Accountability-communication by both sides.

6. Advocating, Facilitating. The coach opens doors for the mentee. The coach requests proactive changes of mentee, evaluates realism of goals, offers truths about path to success and shortcomings of mentee's approaches. Bonded collaboration toward each other's success.

7. Sharing Profound Wisdom. The coach stands for mentees throughout careers, celebrates successes. Energy coaching and love-respect for each other continues throughout the relationship. Mentor actively recruits fellow business colleagues to become mentors. Lifelong dedication toward mentorship...in all aspects of one's life.

Third Party Building Affects Business Climate

Everyone needs a friend to speak on his or her behalf. When things get tough, it's nice to have someone to count on.

Companies--like individuals--must bank support. Times to call for endorsements inevitably arise. The time to build bridges is today...not when crisis strikes.

In selling goods and services, third party support may include past and present clients, suppliers and industries affected by your customers.

In affecting policies and disposition toward your doing business, liaisons must be established with elected officials, the judiciary, regulatory agencies, the public sector, advocate groups and private sector opinion makers.

Most companies realize the impact of special-publics community support, including various socio-economic and ethnic groups. Cause-related marketing, environmental sensitivity and meaningful "giving back to the community" are essential for the coming years.

These recommendations are offered for gaining and maintaining third party endorsements:

- Make lists of your company's current friends and enemies. Update them regularly.

- Determine why friends support you...and what would happen if their backing was lost.

- Understand why some people and groups oppose you. Ascertain what would have prevented their objections and what it would take to turn them around.

- List whom you want to win as friends and with whom you are most afraid of becoming enemies.

- Analyze what your competitors are doing to win friends and build coalitions.

- Foresee what would happen if you sat still and did nothing.

- Project the financial and other benefits of proactive building of credible third party endorsements.

- Make this initiative a primary responsibility for top management.

- Retain outside counsel with demonstrated expertise in issues management and forecasting, community relations, cause-related marketing, minority relations, government relations and grassroots constituency building.

Third party support can move mountains when you need it the most...or it can wreak havoc on your bottom line and the future in which you do business. Be honest about your current status. Take stock of opportunities. Make decisive actions, and reap future rewards.

Business Advisory Boards

Every company needs objective input on the business climate. With informed perspective, management can chart future growth and compete in a changing marketplace.

Non-profit organizations learned long ago the importance of assembling collective expertise. Boards, advisory councils, development committees and other volunteer structures contribute to organizational effectiveness. Successful non-profits seek to routinely upgrade the calibre of resources and to maximize their use.

Similarly, the private sector can muster ideas via Business Advisory Councils.

Some corporations form committees, with regular meetings. Business leaders from industries significant to company success are recruited. Honorariums are paid for participation: by the hour, deal-effecting ability or agreed retainer for advice and counsel.

Small and mid-sized businesses collect independent thought by retaining management consultants. Qualified public relations counsel brings that expertise. PR counsel can then assemble others "spheres of influence," including community and business leaders.

Business Advisory Councils must be chartered with defined purposes: strategic planning, product development, marketing, staff development, joint venturing, industry dominance or otherwise. Choose feasible goals in the beginning. Expand council scope as results are realized.

Everyone needs support. No business is an island unto itself.

The Big Picture of Small and Emerging Businesses

82% of all the companies in America are small and emerging businesses. 98% of all new business starts are small and emerging businesses.

The primary categories of emerging businesses are: (1) Retail. (2) Build a new mousetrap. (3) Clone mousetraps. (4) Pursue a dream that was started elsewhere. (5) Transition company...nurturing to grow and then sell to someone else. (6) Just for the bucks. (7) Professional services.

The realistic life expectancies are that 66.7% of all businesses cannot grow any further than they are now. 44.1% of all companies should not grow into large organizations. 36.2% have limited life expectancies and are destined to be acquired by a larger organization.

I've talked with many entrepreneurs and founders of companies which rapidly grew from the seed of an idea they had. Most admitted enjoying the founding phase but lost interest shortly after giving birth. Over and over, they said, "When it stops being fun, I move on."

After the initial honeymoon, you speak with them and hear rumblings like, "It isn't supposed to be this hard. Whatever happened to the old days? I'm ready to move on. This seems too much like running a business. I'm an idea person, and all this administrative stuff is a waste of my time. I should move on to other new projects."

When they come to me, they want the business to transition smoothly and still make the founders some money. They ask, "Are you the one who comes in here and looks after my interests?"

I reply, "No. After the caretakers come in and apply the wrong approaches to making something of your business, I'm the one who cleans up after them and starts the business over again." The reality is that I'm even better on the front end, helping business owners avoid the costly pitfalls attached to their losing interest and abdicating to the wrong people.

Most companies enjoy the early stage of success...and wish things would stay as in the beginning. When "the fun ends," the hard work begins.

It is crucial for principals of the emerging business to follow their dreams, develop a cohesive Strategic Plan, find a niche and stay with the program sufficiently long to measure results.

These are the mindsets that will sabotage the success of small businesses: (1) Categorically don't want to grow. (2) Growth is all that matters. (3) Company leaders are not good at networking. (4) Company representatives can sell well but follow through delivery suffers. (5) Take the unrealistic premise technology is all that matters. (6) Executives don't like to sell...but need to realize that every executive must contribute to business development.

These are the 7 Basics of Small Business Growth Strategy, per categories on my trademarked business concept, The Business Tree™ :

1. The business you're in. Clear understanding of what the business really is and why you've got what the target marketplace needs and wants.

2. Running the business. Core industry people must learn how to be managers. Give administrative team enough rein-resources to do their jobs. Insist upon a wholistic relationship to the rest of the tree-organization.

3. Financial. Financial managers-personnel-consultants must focus beyond their own niche. Profit cannot be the only driving force. Show-measure full accountability.

4. People. The largest, most overlooked branch of the tree-organization. Employees must be empowered. Management must develop people skills. Job descriptions, evaluations and advancements are documented-communicated. Train regularly.

5. Business Development. Do all things neces-

sary to capture-maintain market share. Maintain sales, marketing, advertising, public relations, research and product development programs...which must interact cohesively with each other.

6. Body of Knowledge. Understand the relationship of each branch to the other. Research-know what's going on outside your doors. Develop the tools to change.

7. The Big Picture. Business cannot grow without a wholistic relationship to all parts of the tree-organization...what benefits one department benefits all. Keep existing roots living and sprout deeper, healthier ones (long-term planning). Master change. Shared Vision must be crafted, articulated and followed.

These are the 7 biggest roadblocks to Emerging Business Growth, per categories on The Business Tree™:

1. The business you're in. Not clear about the business you're really in, much less how-when-why to grow. Growth just for the sake of growth can ruin what you've built.

2. Running the business. Not properly trained or equipped to handle rapid influxes of business. Production, deliverability strained already... and it gets worse.

3. Financial. Increased revenues, new sales and

heightened profits are the only driving forces, without understanding how to protect the business you already have.

4. People. Employees are taught that corporate growth is the most important objective. Not empowered to make decisions or take risks. Management appears distant, with limited people skills. Employees don't really associate with company Vision because they're not sure what it is or what's in it for them.

5. Business Development. Customer service suffers the most. Company is likely to be killing the goose that laid the golden egg.

6. Body of Knowledge. Management doesn't take the time to understand how the company has grown or analyze the relationship of each branch to the other. Setting themselves up to avoid change...yet grow without a Vision.

7. The Big Picture. Business will not grow because no Big Picture ever existed. Cannot truly grow without a crafted Vision for the future.

What If These Things Occur?
per categories on The Business Tree™ :

1. The business you're in.

- You are really in the correct business-industry.

- The product-service is really the best it can be.
- Customers get from your company what they cannot get elsewhere.

2. Running the business.

- The company is properly structured to do the job demanded.
- Operations are sound, professional and productive. Technology is used wisely.
- The physical plant is enough to do the job and can accommodate growth.
- Products-services are delivered on schedule.

3. Financial.

- Keeping the cash register ringing is not the only reason for being in business.
- You always give customers their money's worth. Your charges are fair and reasonable.
- Business is run economically and efficiently. Employees have fiduciary responsibility.

4. People.

- Your company is people-friendly.
- Executives possess good people skills.

- Staff is professional, empowered, likeable and competent.

- Employees demonstrate initiative and use their best judgment, with authority to make the decisions they should make.

- You provide a good place to work. You offer a promising career and future for people with ideas and talent. Your people do a good day's work for a day's pay.

5. Business Development.

- The company always researches and serves the marketplace.

- Customer service is efficient and excellent. You are sensitive to customers' needs and are flexible and human in meeting them.

- You don't market or sell anything that is not true or can be delivered.

- Sales and company operations communicate with each other.

- Your company and its products-services really do have a Point of Difference.

6. Body of Knowledge.

- You develop-champion the tools to change.

- There is a sound understanding of the relationship of each business function to the other.

- You maintain a well-earned reputation and are awake to company obligations.

- You provide leadership for progress, rather than following along.

7. The Big Picture.

- The organization and its components approach business as a Body of Work...a lifetime track record of accomplishments.

- You have and regularly update-benchmark a strategy for the future, shared company Vision, ethics, Big Picture thinking and "walk the talk."

In the average company, many of these things do not occur because:

- People do not know the processes to enable them to occur.

- Rigid adherence to egos and the old ways precludes success.

- The wrong people are giving advice and have the ear of top management.

- Management is out of touch and ego-driven

to lead without proper help or advice.

- The company does not feel that it needs to change...that change is something that others need, but not them.

- Perceptions of current success overshadow the hint that winds will shift in business.

- Assumptions are false and overshadow reality.

- The company is not really in the right business anyway.

- Management is afraid to think "outside the box."

- The company culture is based simply upon being afraid...and paralyzed to do anything new, creative or pro-active.

Every business, company or organization goes through cycles in its life. At any point, each program or business unit is in a different phase from others. The astute organization assesses the status of each program and orients its team members to meet constant changes and fluctuations.

Strategic Planning facilitates disciplined thinking about the organization, its environment and its future. It identifies conflicts, reinforces team building and serves as a vehicle for monitoring organizational progress.

The planning process is then translated into a company Vision. With that Vision, the organization will evolve steadily toward success. Without any kind of Vision, management will continually apply corrective techniques ("band-aid surgery"), while the company stumbles and falls. The price tag for false surgery is six times that of front-end Vision...a concept that I call The High Cost of Doing Nothing™ .

To "go the distance," the organization must complete all seven stages of evolution. There are no fast-forward buttons or skipping steps in developing an effective organization, just as there are no shortcuts in formulating a career and Body of Work.

19

Reference-Appendix

Unexpected Sources of Practical Education, Expressions, Unearthed Information, Trivia

Odd But Truisms

No matter how much planning one does (which I strongly advocate and facilitate for clients), many things just happen. Accidents that work are called strokes of genius.

Daily business is shaped by eccentricities, external influences and chance occurances. By studying some of them, we gain insight into what modern business could be.

During a visit to the United States in the 1960's, Soviet Premier Nikita Khrushchev placed his hand on the tail fin of a Cadillac limousine. With seeming innocence, he asked, "What does this thing do?"

Eliot and Ruth Handler founded a toy company known as Mattel, Inc. They had a daughter named Barbie, who played with paper dolls, pretending that she was a mommy. Ruth watched her child play and got the idea for a doll with accessories, pretending to be an independent adult. Thus was born the largest selling doll in the history of the world...the Barbie Doll.

For those wondering the practical applications of outer space technology and research, look to items now normally found in the home, notably pocket calculators and microwave ovens.

So many odd-but-true happenings created the lifestyle that the populace embraced. Pop art, inventions, fashions, fads, and natural obsessions have contributed more to molding a society than textbook lessons. Historians continue to ponder the effects of pop culture.

As times change, the nature of nostalgia changes. While it is fun to remember the old days, we realize that pop art and culture set the rules by which we live as adults. Each generation relates to different phases of pop culture.

In 1965, a young woman in New York suggested to her boyfriend, a printer, that he make posters with Humphrey Bogart's picture. He acquired a negative for free, bought some cheap paper, and printed a batch of posters. Next, he ran a few ads to promote the pop-art posters.

Some kids came into a Greenwich Village bookstore, inquiring about the Bogart posters. The owner found the printer and bought his supply. The printer left town for a long weekend. When he returned, the phone was ringing. The bookstore had sold more than 1,000 Bogart posters, and could they have more. Realizing they were sitting on a goldmine, the printer and the bookstore owner formed Personality Posters. Thus, the celebrity poster boom began.

The atomic bomb is responsible for many societal reactions and phenomena...the most surprising being the bikini bathing suit. Rumors spread during post-World War II testings that the world would end soon.

Fashion designers scheduled the "ultimate" show with the most daring styles. One model shocked the world by wearing a skimpy two-piece suit. The costume—now accepted swimwear—was named for Bikini Atoll, location of bomb testings.

President John F. Kennedy was asked by a *Life Magazine* reporter for a list of his favorite books. Kennedy was a known intellectual who reportedly read one book every day. When the list included the Ian Fleming novel, *From Russia With Love*, the James Bond spy story craze hit America.

Hungarian design professor Erno Rubik devised a multi-colored puzzle in the mid-1970's. Each of six sides has nine squares, with each row able to rotate around its center. When solved, each side is one color. There are 43 quintillion possible positions. The least possible moves necessary to solve is 20. Rubik's Cube sold billions of units in its heyday. Knowledge of group theory and algorithms is useful.

Witness these fabulous firsts: The first product to carry the union seal was the cigar (1874). Franz Schubert wrote 1,000 musical works but left only one symphony unfinished. Ohio is the birth state of the most U.S. Presidents (seven). The last teenager to rule England was Queen Victoria.

People possess and vigorously demonstrate a passion for trivia. Stored nuggets of information may burst from the memory banks at any given time.

We can recite lyrics to golden oldies on the radio, yet the tenets of business etiquette are not so familiar. We remember movie dialog and old TV advertising jingles, yet policies and procedures are a little foreign.

It is the intention of this book to merge the familiar with the meaningful. Media analogies help readers to connect with their own field of reference. Futurism and cutting edge philosophies have a basis in the familiar.

What They Say, How They Behave

We live in a society filled with contradictions. People say they experience the good life but list concerns and traumas. They say they want creative improvisation but, alas, are creatures of habit and will steadfastly defend the status quo.

Many acknowledge defects in the system but are generally pleased with it. The process of change (which is 90% positive) puts great scare in the population. All of this affects their behavior, attitude, productivity and commitment to business organizations.

To give further complexity to the ways in which businesses are reflective of and affected by societal dynamics, here is what some of the research shows:

74% of Americans keep money in their wallet, pocketbook and pocket...sorted in order of denomination.

68% of Americans lick the flap of an envelope from left to right.

47% of the population wear eye glasses of some type.

8% of all Americans receive food stamps.

79% of all adults are missing at least one tooth.

48% of Americans apply extra salt to their food. Of those who do, 34% apply it before ever tasting the food (out of habit).

95% of American unskilled laborers are generally satisfied with their life. 82% of all unemployed Americans are generally satisfied with their lives.

14% of all families own a business.

Alaska accounts for 16% of the American land mass.

74% of all adults have a high school diploma.

82% of Americans think it is OK to cheat on income taxes, to some extent.

20% of all 6th graders cannot locate the United States on a map.

76% of small business owners do not have a college degree.

68% of Americans do not like to take chances.

11% of companies provide child care assistance to their employees.

91% of airline passengers use discounted fares.

3% of all households purchase baby food.

76% of the population has not exercised within the last 24 hours.

29% of the work force wants their boss' job.

67% of the country went to bed before midnight last night.

40% of 5th graders have felt peer pressure to try an alcoholic beverage.

The only symbolic character known to 100% of young children is Santa Claus. Second is Ronald McDonald, who holds a 96% recognition quotient.

11% of citizens over 50 wish they could again be teenagers. 23% think their greatest achievements are still ahead of them past age 50.

Beer accounts for 85% of the alcoholic beverage consumption.

99% of American women think that contributing to or bettering society is important. 35% of Americans are involved in community service and charity activities.

If given the chance, 55% of the population say they would travel into outer space.

63% of American men do housework on a regular basis. 64% of working mothers regularly do after-dinner cleanup without any help from the family.

70% of corporate CEOs think that business and industry are too much focused on the short-term.

75% of American women wear the wrong sized bras.

98% of all new business starts are small businesses. 45% of small business owners are children of small business owners.

83% of all domestic companies have fewer than 20 employees. Only 7% of all companies have 100 or more employees.

3% of all Americans think that George Washington was history's most exciting figure. The same percentage think that Elvis Presley was history's most exciting figure.

5% of all Americans think that John F. Kennedy was history's most exciting figure. The same percentage think that Jesus Christ was history's most exciting figure.

68% of all high school students do not know when the Civil War took place.

5% of all Americans go to McDonald's every day.

50% of the population reads books. 50% do not.

52% of the population daydreams about being rich.

64% of microwave oven owners use the appliance only for warming up items.

How Things Happen and Why...Questions and Curiosities

How many senses do human beings really have?

12 --- taste, smell, hearing, touch, sight, pain, warmth, cold, muscle expansion and contraction, hunger, thirst, equilibrium-balance.

Do all nails grow at the same pace?

No. Fingernails grow twice as fast as toenails.

What animal makes the strongest glue?

The barnacle.

When does a hill become a mountain?

After it surpasses 1,000 feet in height.

Why are computer keyboards structured as they are?

When designing the first production typewriter in 1873, the letters were arranged alphabetically. This caused jamming when bars were on the upstrike. The still-used configuration affords fingers the best agility.

Where did cowboys originate?
Tory irregulars in the Hudson River Valley of New York, during the Revolutionary War.

How do police officers estimate the size of crowds at special events?
Percentage of community population. Density per block. Amount of garbage picked up.

Why are cities warmer than their outlying areas?
Buildings, pavement, factory activity, vehicles, exhaust fumes, lighting, technology. Rain has a cooling effect in the country. Precipitation dries and causes steam in cities.

Why are movie copyrights in Roman numerals?
It just started that way. Nobody changed it. By default, it became a tradition.

What's the best way to kill a rat?
Put out chocolate to entice it. Leave a saucer of beer. The rat will explode because it cannot burp.

When are streets the slickest?
During the first few minutes of a rainstorm, causing skids. Afterward, moisture dries the streets.

What makes a car battery go dead?
Lack of being started often enough, or too much

drainage on electrical cells.

Why is Tuesday designated as election day?
It was arbitrarily picked during the Revolutionary War era and just stuck. Later, it was ratified and, by default, became a custom. Only 1% of the population say that Tuesday is their favorite day of the week.

How many types of energy are there?
12 --- kinetic, mechanical, heat, chemical, electrical, solar, light, potential, muscular, steam, atomic-nuclear, gravitational.

What is the most lucrative casino game?
Blackjack, which accounts for 49% of all casino game winnings.

When did Robin Hood live?
He was a myth. So was The Lone Ranger and his cousin, The Green Hornet (named John Reid and Britt Reid, respectively).

What spurred invention of the phonograph?
Thomas Edison was trying to invent the dictaphone, a piece of business equipment. He later realized that his invention had primarily entertainment implications.

What is the significance of radio station call letters, beginning with K and W?
Stations west of the Mississippi begin with K, and those east of the river begin with W, except for a few on either coast which were grandfa-

thered in. KW is an abbreviation chosen by engineers. KW stands for kilowatt, the measure of power output.

Why are policemen called COPs?
COP is an abbreviation for an English term, Constable on Patrol.

The average person walks 18,000 steps per day.

There are no punctuation marks in alphabet soup.

E is the letter most used in the English language. Next, in order of frequency, are **T**, **A**, **O**, **I** and **N**.

The species with the highest reproductive cycle is the termite, at 1,800 times per year. Other species (not in direct descending order) are the praying mantis (850 times per year), Rabbit (28/year), mink (7/year), humming bird (2/year) and the elephant (once every two years).